Love to Sew

Leinennähmaschinenzwirn
Extra prima Qualität
Drei-fach
30
POLYESTER

Love to Sew
60 STUNNING ACCESSORIES TO MAKE FOR YOU AND YOUR HOME
SEARCH PRESS

The projects in this book have been made using metric measurements, and the imperial equivalents provided have been calculated following standard conversion practices. The imperial measurements are often rounded to the nearest ⅛in for ease of use. If you need more exact measurements, there are a number of excellent online converters that you can use. Always use either metric or imperial measurements, not a combination of both.

First published in 2021

Search Press Limited
Wellwood, North Farm Road,
Tunbridge Wells, Kent TN2 3DR

This book uses material from the following books in the *Love to Sew* series published by Search Press:

Hanging Hearts, 2012, Rachael Rowe
Mug Rugs, 2013, Christa Rolf
Patchwork Bags, 2013, Cecilia Hanselmann
Zakka-Style Gifts, 2014, Cecilia Hanselmann
Vintage-Style Gifts for the Home, 2014, Christa Rolf
Simple Patchwork Gifts, 2014, Christa Rolf
Little Bags & Purses, 2015, Saskia Abel
Christmas Stockings, 2015, Rachael Rowe
Quilted Covers & Cosies, 2015, Debbie Shore
Quick & Easy Patchwork, 2016, Claudia Schmidt
Sewing Room Accessories, 2016, Debbie Shore
Lagom-Style Accessories, 2018, Debbie von Grabler-Crozier
Quilting on the Move, 2019, Alistair Macdonald

Photographs by Uwe Blick, Paul Bricknell, Uli Glasemann, Stacy Grant, Garie Hind, Debbie Patterson, Elke Reith, Karin Schlag, Birgit Völkner & Atelier Lichtwechsel

ISBN: 978-1-78221-792-3

SUPPLIERS

If you have difficulty in obtaining any of the materials and equipment mentioned in this book, then please visit the Search Press website for details of suppliers: www.searchpress.com

Contents

INTRODUCTION

Is your stash pile growing faster than you can handle? Are you looking for inspiring and creative ways to use it up and make useful, unique items for your home, or for friends and family? If so, this book will give you 60 very good reasons to bust out your sewing machine and get creative!

Featuring the very best of the popular *Love to Sew* series, this book contains 60 exciting projects, including placemats, purses and pillows, along with bags, baskets and boxes. The projects vary in difficulty, and each is graded one, two or three cottonreels accordingly – one cottonreel being the easiest and three the most complex. There are lots of projects that will appeal to competent beginners and more advanced sewists alike – but don't be afraid to push yourself. Each project offers you a new and inspiring way to use up treasured scraps or modest amounts of much-loved fabrics.

There is a comprehensive techniques section at the start, which ensures that you can either swot up first, or refer back to it later, should you need to. It covers techniques such as making and applying bias binding, adding frills, quilting, adding piping and inserting zips.

Whatever the occasion or whomever the recipient, you are sure to find something suitable here. So put the kettle on, plug in your sewing machine and enjoy some quality you-time! Happy sewing!

Here are a few projects from throughout the book to whet your appetite: purse keyrings, opposite top left (see pages 98–99); oven glove and tea towel set, opposite top right (see pages 86 –89); table runner, top left (see pages 140–141); triple layer cake pincushion, top right (see pages 162–163); cutlery roll, above left (see pages 62–65); hot water bottle cover, above (see pages 150–153), and patchwork coasters, left (see pages 36–37).

Before you start

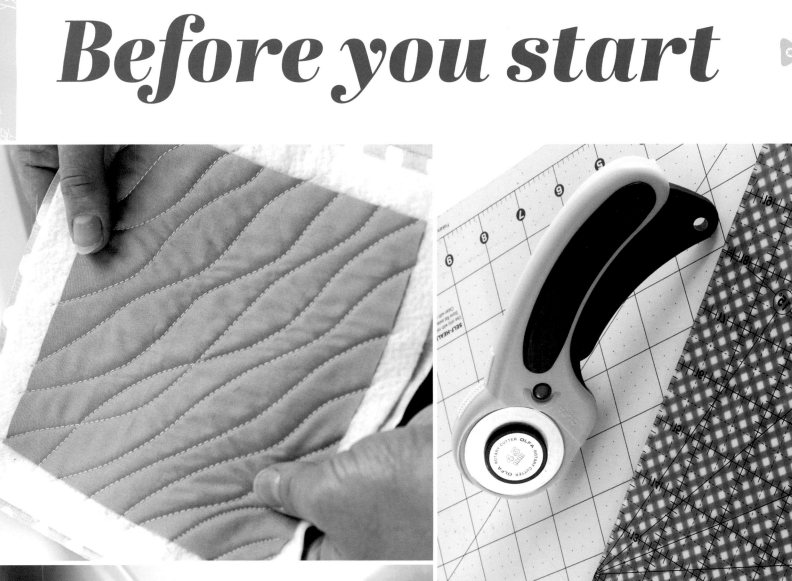

IN YOUR SEWING BOX

You don't need an extensive range of equipment to get started. Pick up a few select items and then build up your kit over time, once you know what you really need.

FABRIC

Buy the best-quality natural fabric that you can, such as 100 per cent cotton fabric. Bear in mind that nylon and polyester or blends can give unpredictable results.

FELT

Avoid the rainbow of acrylic felts available to you. Handmade wool felt in its soft muted hues looks lovely and, probably more importantly, wears better than acrylic types, too.

THREAD

Buy good-quality thread – it will wear well and be a pleasure to sew with. Don't feel you have to own every available shade – buy a few favourite colours to get you started, then add to your collection over time.

INTERFACINGS

These are the foundations of your sewing projects. No one likes a sad and droopy bag, or a quilt that feels like a tablecloth, so get familiar with the different types available and get some for your stash.

HABERDASHERY

Zips, elastics, ribbons and that sort of thing are what make a project come together (and stay together too!). Make your item functional, lovely and long-lasting.

EMBELLISHMENTS

You're likely to have at least a few buttons stashed away at home already, but keep your eyes peeled whenever you shop and pick up bargains or eye-catching favourites, so that they are always to hand when you need them.

SEWING MACHINE

Most of these projects require a sewing machine. You don't need to invest in a top-of-the-range machine – most of the projects only require a straight or zigzag stitch anyway...

SEWING TOOLS

You need the usual suspects: hand-sewing needles, scissors (large for fabric and small for little jobs), a tape measure, pins, a thimble, a quick unpick and so on. These will prove essential on any sewing project.

ADHESIVES

Depending on the project, you may need different types of adhesive: fusible web for attaching appliqué shapes, spray adhesive for securing layers of fabric or wadding/batting, fabric glue for securing zips or wet glue for the odd trim. Always read the instructions carefully, and if the glue is to be stitched through, ensure that it is suitable to go through your machine.

OTHER SPECIAL THINGS...

Most of the time, you can make these projects with a very basic kit and everything will go to plan with no stress. However, there are some things that make life a little easier. Consider these:

ROTARY CUTTER, MAT AND RULER: scissors will do the job, but using a rotary cutter is faster and more accurate.

WATER-SOLUBLE FABRIC MARKER: I could not be without one of these to remind me of essential markings.

BEESWAX: really nice for keeping threads tangle-free.

EMBROIDERY HOOP: for steering your work when sewing free-machine embroidery (see page 19).

BIAS TAPE MAKER: for easier bias tape making and a more professional result (see page 20).

ARTGALLERYFABRICS.COM
DESIGNER RULE
60044

BASIC SEWING TECHNIQUES

Here are a few key techniques and sewing terms that you'll need to be familiar with before you begin.

RIGHT SIDES FACING

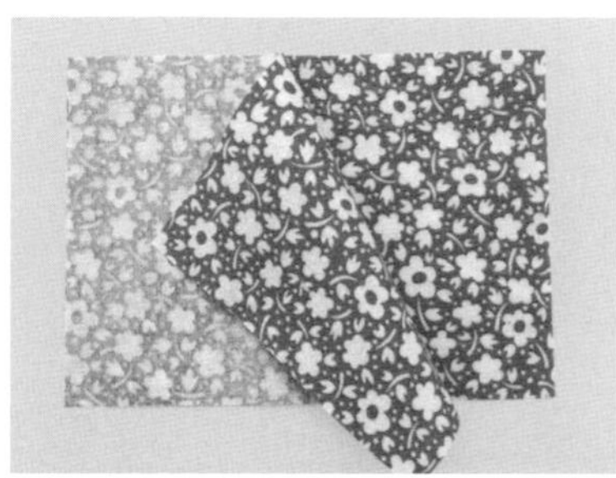

The front of a fabric is known as the 'right side', so it follows that the back is known as the 'wrong side'. If two pieces of fabric are to be sewn together, they are usually placed together with the right sides facing. When turned through after sewing, the seam allowances will then be hidden.

FOOT WIDTH

Unless stated otherwise, fabrics are generally sewn together with a seam allowance of 6mm (¼in). This is also known as a 'foot width', because the right-hand edge of the fabric runs parallel to the right-hand edge of the sewing-machine foot when sewing. However, some sewing feet are narrower or wider, so use the needle position to correct the space between the needle and the right-hand edge of the foot if you need to.

SECURING SEAMS

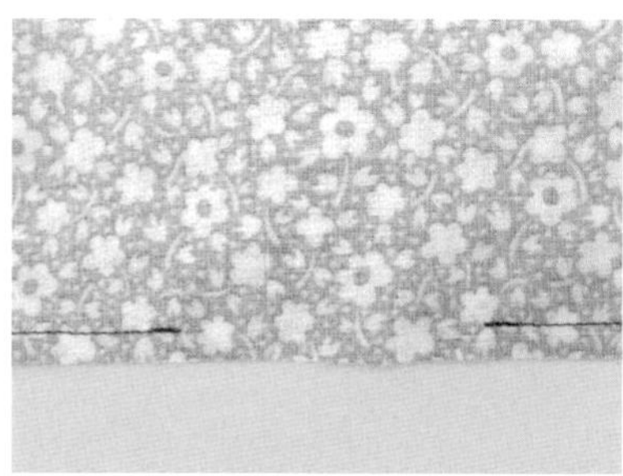

Any seams that are not going to be oversewn again later – for instance at turning openings or visible topstitched seams – need to be 'secured' so that they don't come apart. At the beginning of the seam, sew three or four stitches forwards, then three or four stitches back, then sew forwards again. Do the same at the end of the seam.

CLOSING A TURNING OPENING

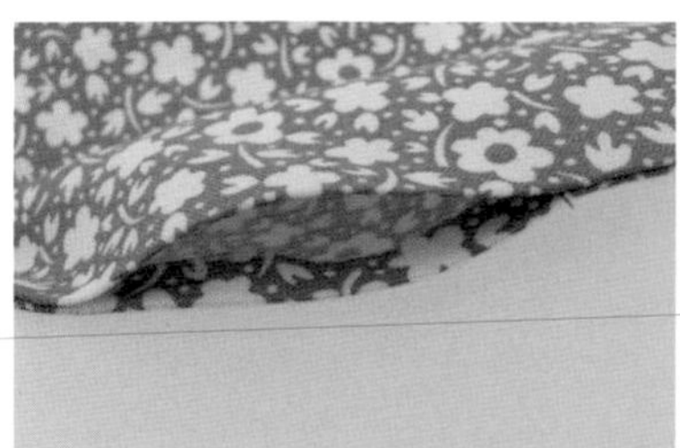

With your project turned right way out, turn the seam allowances to the inside along the turning opening. Sew up the opening by hand using small, discreet hand stitches such as ladder stitch: insert the needle in the folded edge and draw it through again a little further on, then insert in the opposite folded edge at the same level. Continue like this and tighten the thread after a few stitches. Once you have closed the opening, secure the thread neatly.

TURNING OUT CORNERS

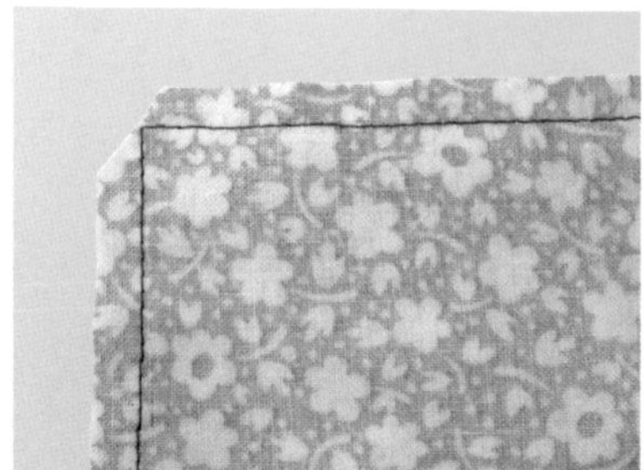

Trim across sewn corners, through the seam allowances close to your stitch line but being careful not to snip your stitches. This will reduce bulk at the corner and ensure the corner sits nicely when it is turned through. When poking out the corners, use a slim, rounded item such as a chopstick, to ensure you don't damage your seams.

TURNING OUT CURVED SHAPES

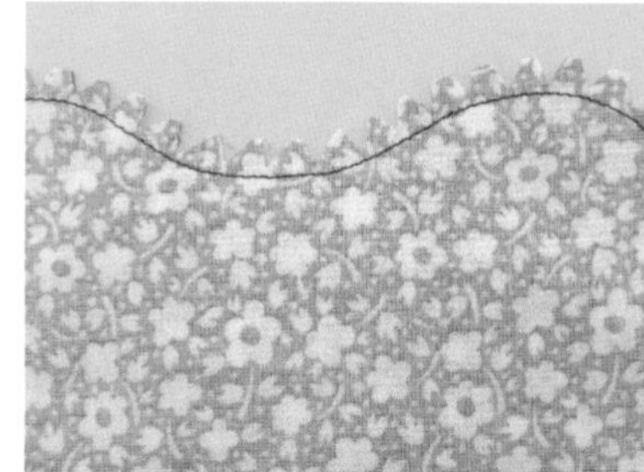

For curved seams, snip tiny triangles into the seam allowances, or use pinking shears. This ensures that the curves will sit nice and flat when the fabric is right side out, as the seam allowance is more evenly distributed between the triangles.

TOPSTITCHING

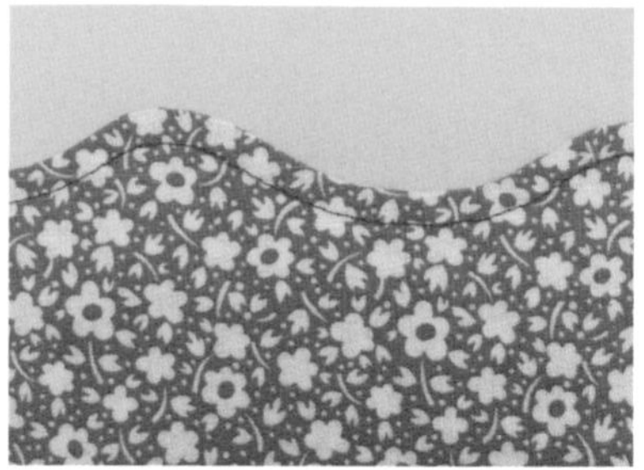

When topstitching a seam, make sure you keep an equal distance from the edge all along the seam. If you are stitching rounded or curved edges, you might want to draw in the line with a self-erasing fabric marker pen first. Edge stitching is similar to topstitching, but usually closer to the fabric edge – about 2–3mm (⅛in) away.

SIMPLE PATCHWORKING

1 When patchworking, always iron both seam allowances to one side together (usually behind a darker fabric, if there is one). If several groups or rows are being sewn together, iron each row's seam allowances in a different direction, so that they will nest together nicely when sewn (see step 2).

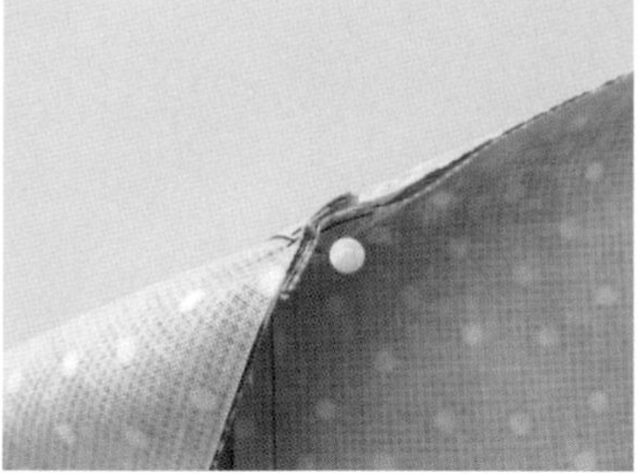

2 The seam allowances that are facing in different directions should 'slide' together in the correct positions. Ensure that the vertical seams are perfectly aligned, secure them with a pin, then sew the edges together.

3 You should end up with neat, perfectly aligned squares. Open out the rows and iron the seam allowances in one direction.

continued...

MAKING TIES/LOOPS

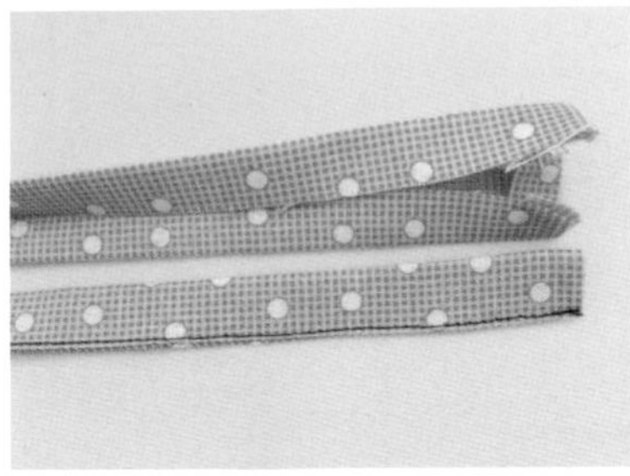

As per your project instructions, fold the strip in half lengthways and iron lightly down the fold. Open the strip out again, then fold the two long sides from the outside to the middle fold and iron. Fold the strips in half and iron well. Fold one short end over to the inside by about 6mm (¼in). Fold the strip again and edge stitch the folded edges neatly.

INSERTING TIES

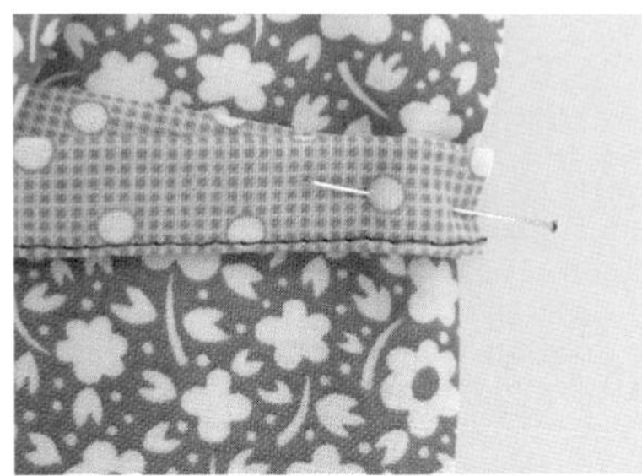

1 Lay the ties on the right side of the fabric with the unfinished ends of the ties at the edge. Place the second piece of fabric on top. Sew along the edge. Make sure the pins securing the ties are out of the way of the seam. If preferred, tack/baste your ties in place before stitching.

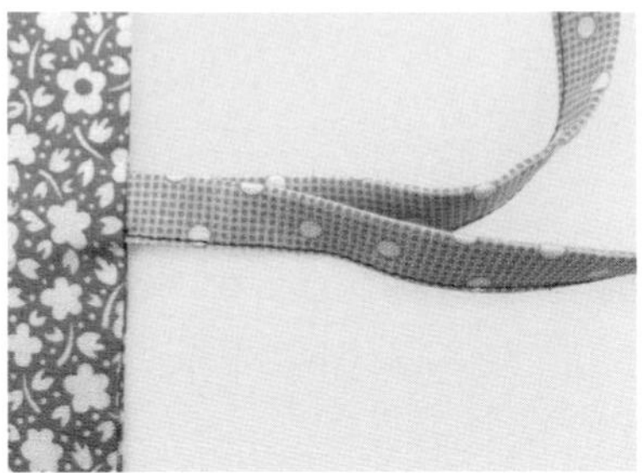

2 When you turn the item right side out, the ties will be on the outside. Be careful not to sew through the loose ends of the ties as you sew up your project!

MAKING A BOX BASE

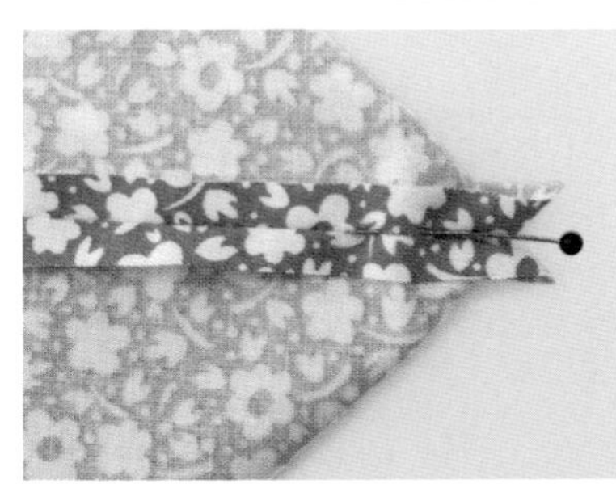

1 Once you have sewn the bottom seam of a bag or pouch, open out the seam allowances and refold the fabric, so that the base seam sits on top of a side seam; pin, as shown.

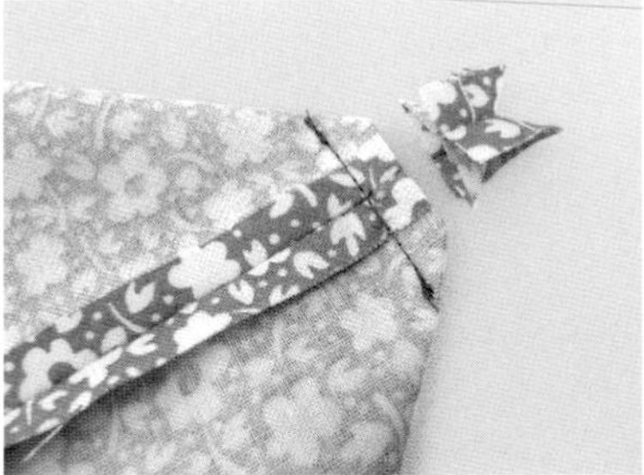

2 Sew across the triangular point at the stated width on both sides, securing the beginning and end well. Trim the triangles back to the width of the seam allowance and neaten.

3 Turn the bag through, right side out, to give the corners their boxed shape.

EMBROIDERY STITCHES

Here are a few simple embroidery stitches that you might need for embellishing some of your projects. Always make sure your thread is secure before stitching, and knot or secure the thread before you cut it, to prevent it coming undone.

RUNNING STITCH

This is one of the easiest stitches of all and it is used a lot in traditional embroidery work. Make sure that you keep an eye on your technique; the trouble with this stitch is that the stitches can get bigger and bigger if you don't watch out. That means unpicking, so it is better to keep stock of what you are doing from the get-go.

Bring the knotted thread up somewhere on the design (A). Instead of going straight down, go down and up through the fabric a few times (B and C) with a rocking motion and then pull the needle – this way you will sew a few running stitches at once. Keep going until you complete your row.

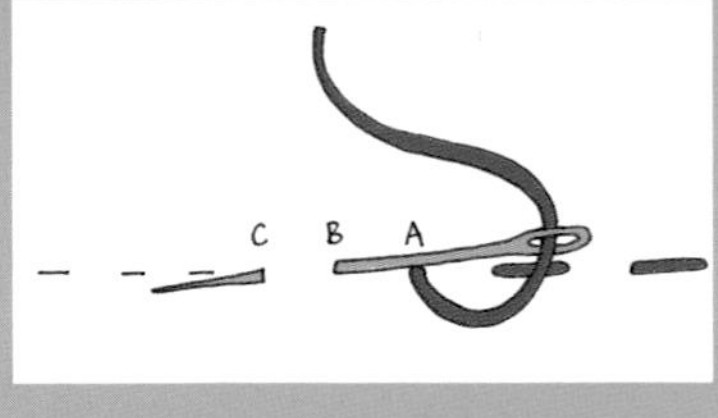

BACKSTITCH

Backstitch is great to learn if you want to create strong lines for outlines or text. Once again, keep it even and if you really have trouble, try marking dots where the stitch should be with your water-soluble marker until you get your eye in.

Begin with your threaded needle and come up from the back of the work (A). Go down at B which, as you can see from the line, is behind A. This is the back bit.

Come back up at point C, which is a little ahead of A. C now becomes the new A, and A is the new B. Go back down again at A (through the same hole, so that you get your unbroken line) and go up through the fabric at D.

Continue in this way until you have the line that you want.

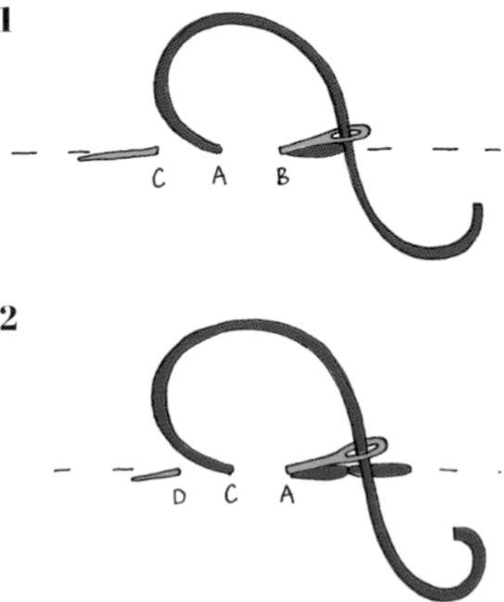

FRENCH KNOT

This is a classic stitch and although there are many ways of making a French knot, this is one of the easiest. You can make the knot larger by wrapping the thread around the needle a few more times.

Begin by bringing the thread up from the back of the work (at A). Wrap the thread around the needle two or three times. Slide your wraps down the needle to make a knot. Take the needle back down near to where you came up (at B), leaving a little knot behind.

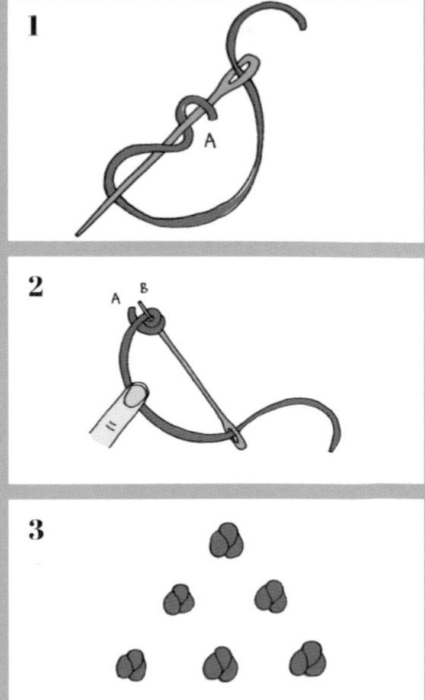

APPLIQUÉ

Appliqué is great for embellishing your work and telling a story with pictures. There are many types of appliqué and first we will look at 'raggy-edged' appliqué; so-called because we don't need to worry about finishing the edges. Fear not: it will not fray because in free-motion embroidery (see opposite) the stitches are very close together, which not only stops your design from fraying but means your work can even survive a wash.

RAGGY-EDGED APPLIQUÉ

1 Prepare your shape and glue it in place with a regular glue stick, repositionable spray adhesive or fusible adhesive – this means it cannot move about and you don't have pins to get in the way.

2 Don't fret about being too neat. Choose an appropriate coloured thread and, coming in from the edge just a bit, sew around the appliqué shape. On larger pieces of fabric go around the edge twice, and on smaller ones just once. Don't worry if your stitch lines don't sit exactly on top of each other – this is what gives the technique its wonderful sketchy finish.

Darning foot

For free-motion embroidery (see opposite).

FREE-MOTION EMBROIDERY

Your machine manual will provide information for your particular model but, essentially, you need to either set the stitch length to zero (older models) or cover or drop the feed dogs – this means moving out of the way the little metal plate with teeth under the needle, which is responsible for pulling the fabric through in one direction only. You are then free to manoeuvre the fabric in all directions.

You may wish to use an ordinary embroidery hoop upside down to give yourself something to 'steer' with. Using a darning or free-motion foot allows you to see and 'steer' more easily.

APPLIQUÉ GALLERY

The different ways you might choose to attach your appliqué shape to your project can give it a very different feel. Satin stitch is a traditional finish, while blanket or blind hem stitch give a pleasingly quirky finish.

To make the application easier, use a repositionable spray fabric adhesive to keep the shapes in place, or iron a sheet of fusible adhesive to the back of the fabric before cutting. Then peel off the paper backing and iron the designs into position.

Satin stitch

If you are machine sewing, form a dense line by shortening your zigzag stitch to make it into a satin stitch. This technique will also help prevent woven fabrics from fraying.

Blanket stitch

Felt or fabric appliqué looks charming when hand-embroidered with blanket or running stitch. Try hand stitching in blanket stitch around woven fabrics too – this gives a rustic look to your work. For a neater look, use the blanket or pin stitch on your sewing machine.

Blind hem stitch

Try your machine's blind hem stitch if you don't want to see very much of the stitching. Always test out the stitch on scrap fabric first, to make sure you are happy with it.

BIAS BINDING

Bias binding is a strip of fabric cut on the diagonal, at a 45-degree angle, which allows a little 'give' so that the fabric stretches around curves without puckering. Use it to give a neat, professional-looking bound edge to your projects.

CREATING BIAS STRIPS

Although bias strips (also referred to as bias binding and bias tape) can be bought in many colours and widths, it's a good idea to make your own, as this is cost-effective and means you can coordinate it with your fabrics. To cut your fabric accurately, you will need a rotary cutter, rectangular ruler and cutting mat.

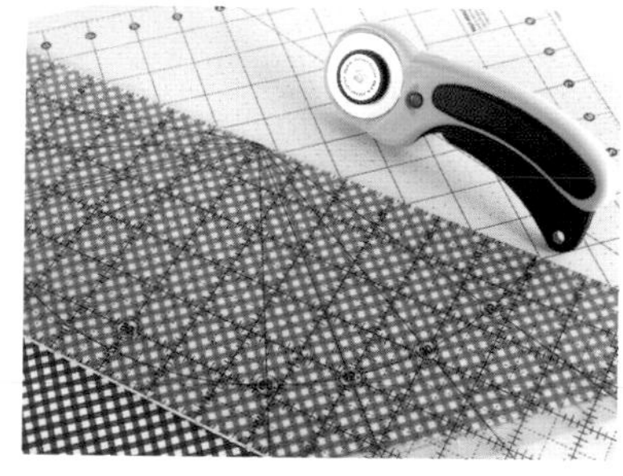

1 Lay your fabric squarely on the cutting mat, and place the 45-degree mark on your ruler on the straight edge of the fabric. Cut along the ruler.

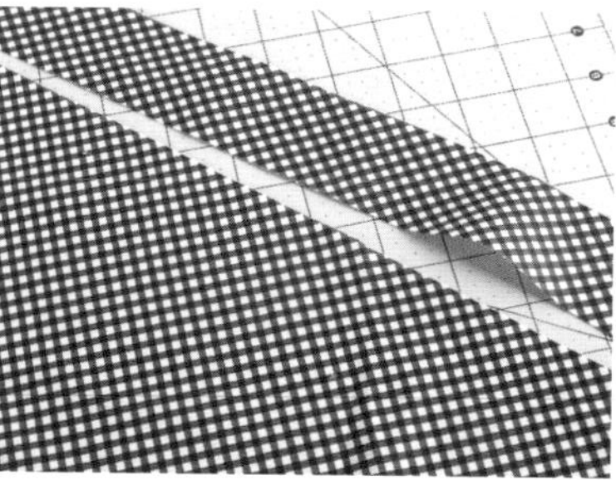

2 Turn your fabric over and use the straight side of the ruler to measure the width you need. For 2.5-cm (1-in) wide bias binding, you need to cut 5-cm (2-in) wide strips of fabric. As you are cutting the strips, the fabric will stretch, so fold it in half diagonally and cut through two, three or four layers at a time.

3 To join the strips, lay two pieces right sides together, overlapping at right angles. Draw a diagonal line from one corner to the other, as in the photograph. Pin, then sew along this line. Trim the raw edge back to around 3mm (⅛in) and then press the seam open.

4 You need to fold both of the long edges of the tape into the centre and press them. The easiest way to do this is to use either a bias binding machine or a small bias-tape maker (shown right). As you pull the strip through this, it folds it in two – press with your iron to fix the folds. If you don't have a tape maker, carefully fold both long edges to the centre of the fabric strip and press. Be careful not to get your fingers too close to the iron!

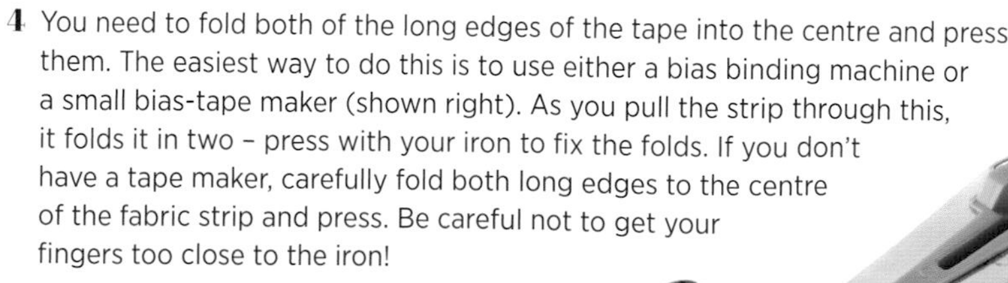

APPLYING BIAS BINDING

Bias binding gives such a neat edge, not only to quilts, but to oven gloves, table mats, handbags and more! A neat, mitred corner really gives a professional finish, and it's not difficult when you know how...

1

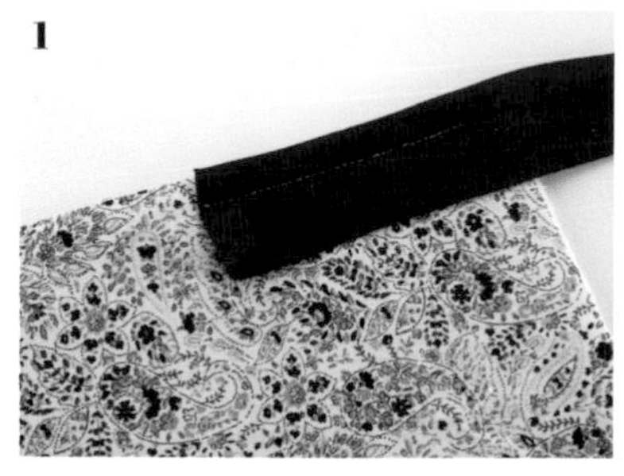

2

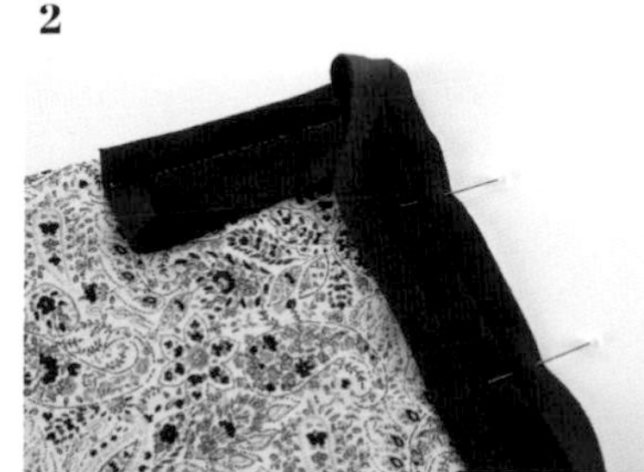

3

4

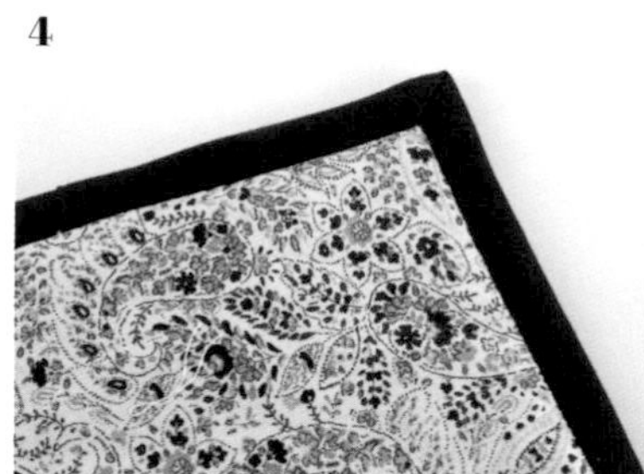

5

6

1 Open out the bias binding and place it right sides together with the edge of your project. Fold in the first end of the binding, as shown. Sew along the crease line but stop 1cm (½in) from the corner and back-tack to stop the stitches coming undone.

2 Take the binding along the second side, making a triangular pleat in the corner. Fold the pleat away from your stitch line, pin in place, and sew along the second side, again stopping 1cm (½in) from the end.

3 Continue in the same way around the next three corners and, when you're back to where you started, overlap the ends of the tape by about 6mm (¼in).

4 Fold the binding over to the back, tucking the folded edge under, and you should see neat mitres forming: mirror the same mitres on the reverse. I like to use fabric clips to hold the edge in place, as the fabric is now quite thick for pinning.

5 Sew the bias binding in place by hand with slip stitch, making sure your machine stitch line is covered by the binding.

6 When you're finished, you'll have really neat, square corners both from the front of your work...

7 ... and from the back!

QUILTING TECHNIQUES

There are countless quilting techniques to choose from, but these three are each attractive in their own right, and will provide inspiration for you to try out your own ideas.

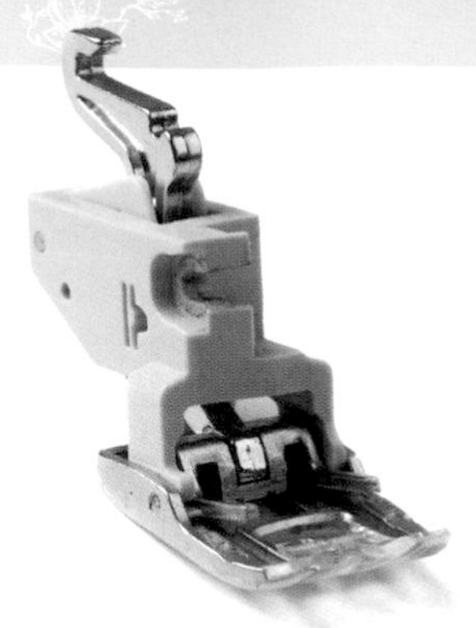

Walking foot
This minimizes fabric shift for quilting projects and designs that have multiple or thick layers (also called an even-feed foot).

FREE-MOTION WAVE QUILTING

This free-motion wave pattern is entirely random; not only is this much easier to sew on your machine than a formal design, it also means that no one can look at your quilt and say that the stitching is wrong!

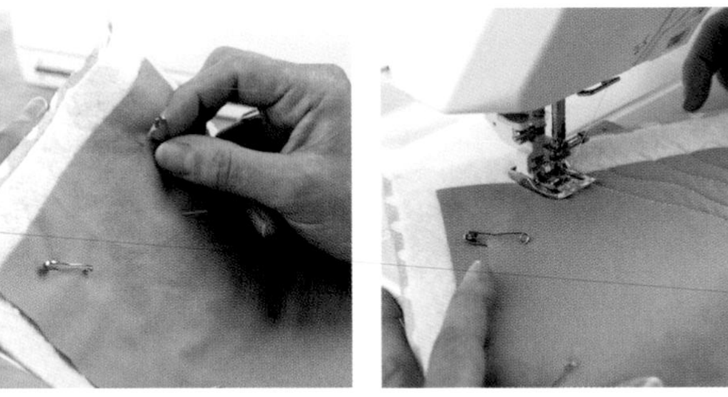

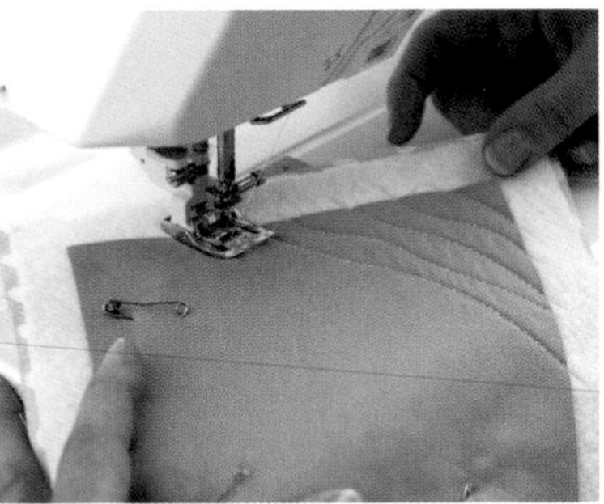

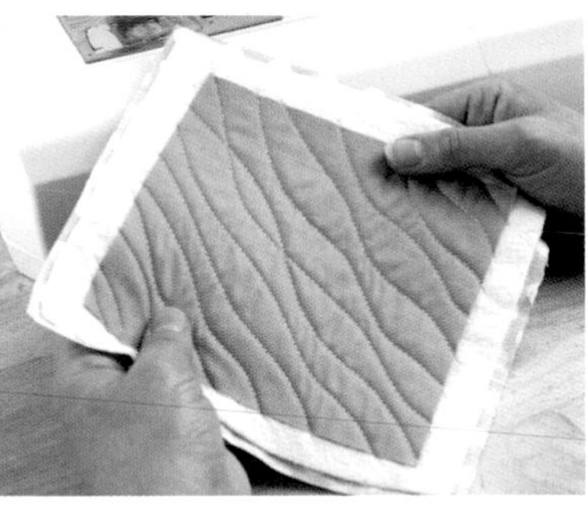

1 Make your quilt sandwich, which means placing your backing and wadding/batting face down, and then the top fabric face up in the centre. Pin the layers together so that no movement is possible (you may want to hand-tack/baste them together instead if you're working on a larger project).

2 Attach a walking foot to your machine and begin quilting with a wavy line. Now turn the fabric and make another wavy line running roughly parallel to the first.

3 Keep going until you have lots of wavy lines; you can keep them all separate, or overlap some of them if you like.

Tip

Always make the wadding/batting and the backing fabric slightly larger than your main fabric, because the three layers will move around and creep slightly as you sew. You won't always need to apply backing fabric, but the quilting technique is the same.

QUILT-AS-YOU-GO

This fun technique allows you to apply fabrics directly to a backing/lining fabric and, by stitching and flipping them, create a wonderful quilted finish in one easy step.

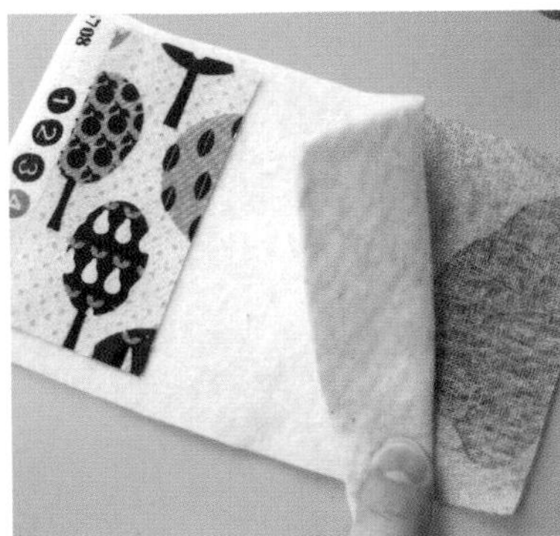

1 Place the backing/lining fabric right side down and place the wadding/batting on top. Position the first patchwork strip on top of it, right side up, at the left-hand side.

2 Place the second patchwork strip, right sides facing and right-hand edges matching, on top of the first one and sew through all the layers, taking a 6mm (¼in) seam allowance.

3 Fold the second strip over so that the right side is showing, then press the seam in place.

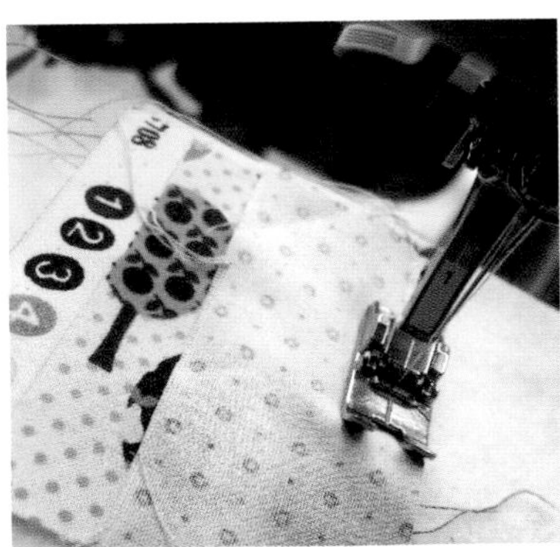

4 Repeat steps 2 and 3, positioning the third strip on top of the second strip, and so on, until you have sewn all the strips together as desired.

5 This is what the patchwork looks like when it has not yet been trimmed to the required size.

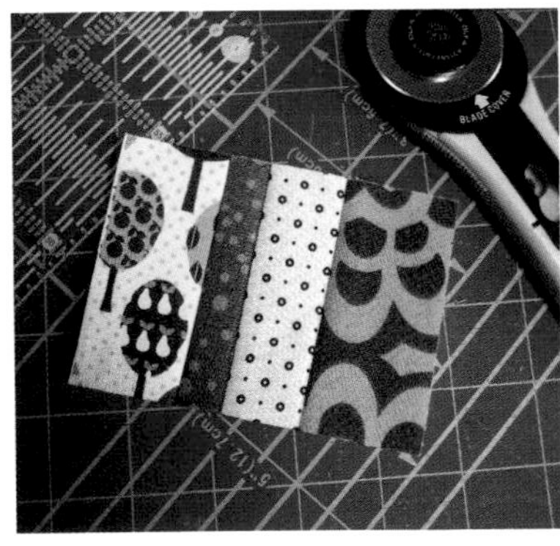

6 Trim the patchwork to the desired dimensions, ideally using a patchwork ruler and a rotary cutter on a cutting mat.

ENGLISH PAPER PIECING

English paper piecing (or EPP) is the technique of folding fabric pieces over paper templates and hand-sewing them together. The paper template shape stabilizes the fabric, ensures that the patchwork shapes are accurate and also makes it easier to piece the angles together. You need only a few items to get started: paper or card templates, fabric, scissors, a needle and some thread.

1 Cut the required number of shapes (here, hexagons) out of card or paper. Place one of the shapes on the fabric and mark around it with tailor's chalk or a fabric marker pen, leaving room for a seam allowance.

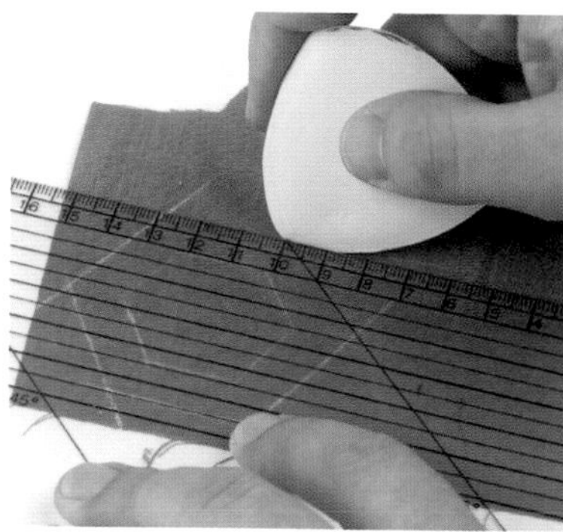

2 Next, mark out a seam allowance around the shape of approximately 1cm (½in).

3 Cut around the outer (seam allowance) line with a pair of sharp fabric scissors. You can now use this fabric piece as a pattern to cut out more, as required.

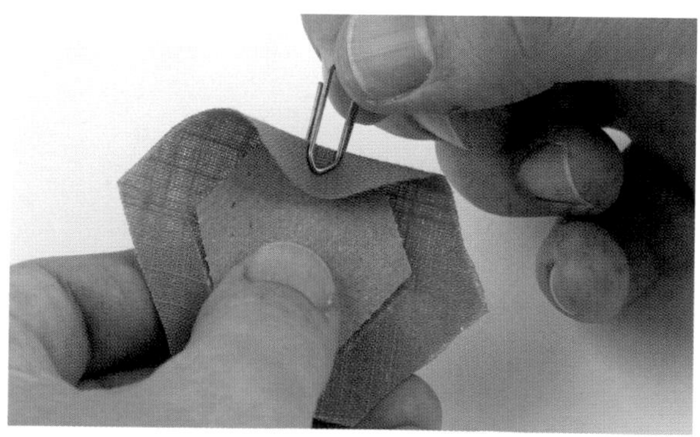

4 Place the card hexagon back in the centre of the fabric and use a paper clip to fold over the seam allowance edge and hold it securely.

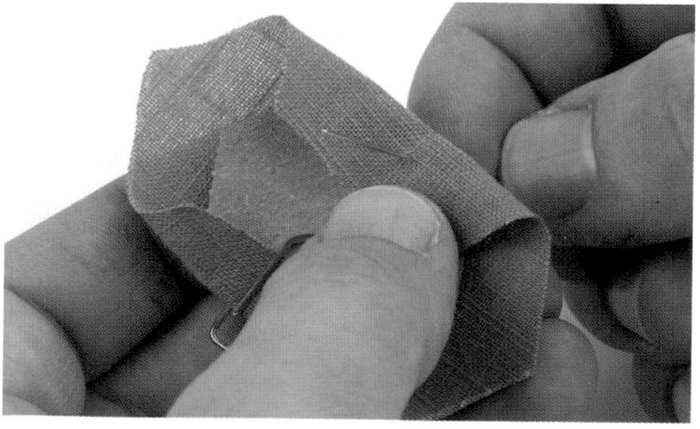

5 Fold over the opposite edge and bring your needle through from front to back using a fairly large tacking/basting stitch.

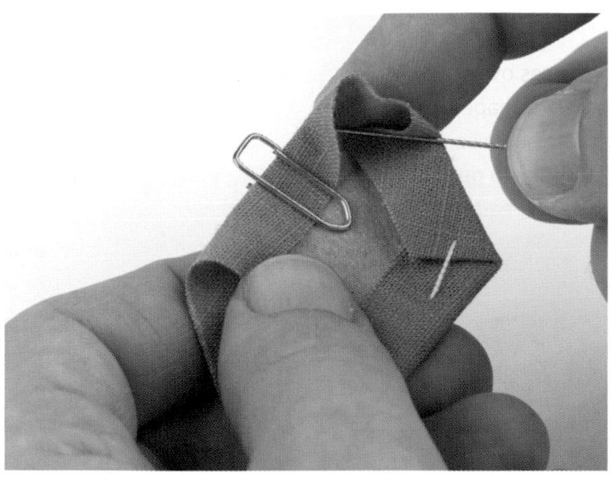

6 Work around the shape, using your needle to achieve a nice, crisp fold, and tack/baste the edges all the way around, catching each fold with your stitches.

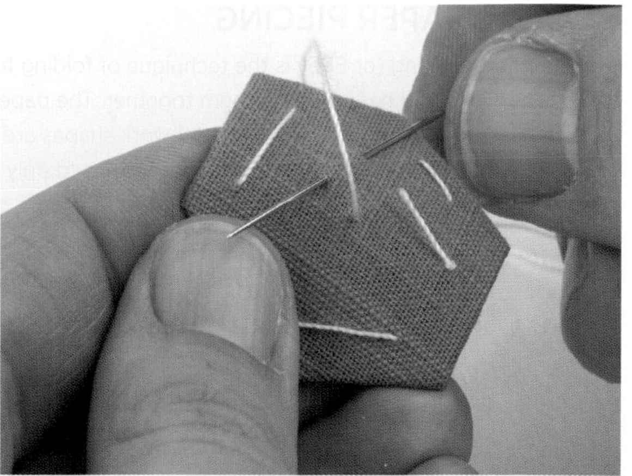

7 When you have tacked/basted the whole shape, take your needle out through the middle and cut the thread. Repeat to create the desired number of shapes.

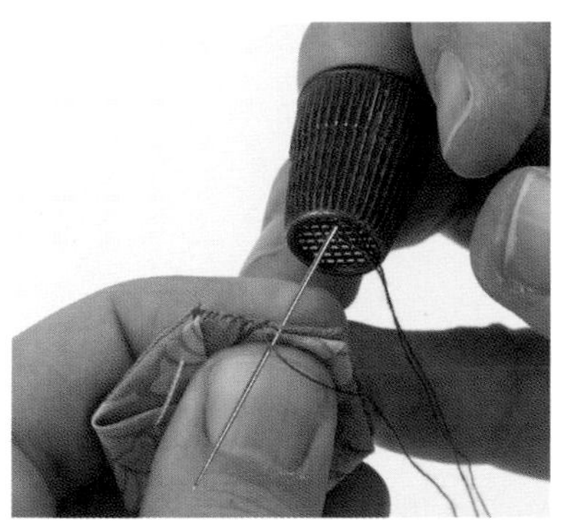

8 To sew your shapes together, hold them with right sides facing and whip stitch them together along one edge only at a time, working through both layers of fabric.

9 Continue to attach them as your pattern dictates (here, in a flower shape), making sure the corners fit together neatly.

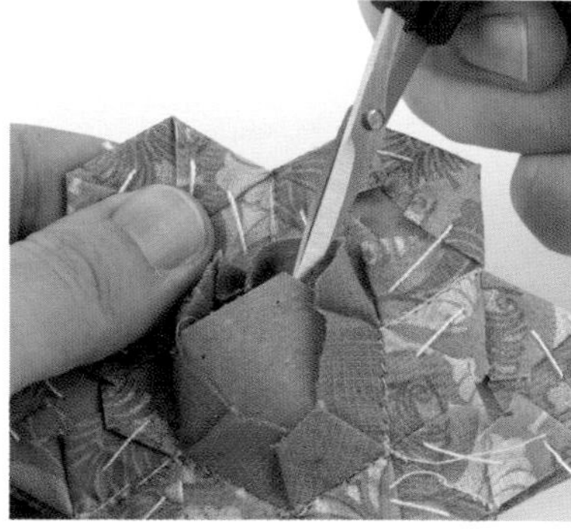

10 Before you sew up your patchwork, take out the tacking/basting stitches and remove all the card/paper shapes.

FINISHING TOUCHES

These essential techniques will add a professional-looking touch to your projects and are simple to do with a bit of practice!

INSERTING A ZIP

Zips needn't be intimidating, as the process isn't all that tricky – it's just very important to temporarily tack/baste the zip into position and test it first before sewing it. There is nothing worse than machining straight away, only to find that the zip is not properly aligned, and then having to unpick it!

1

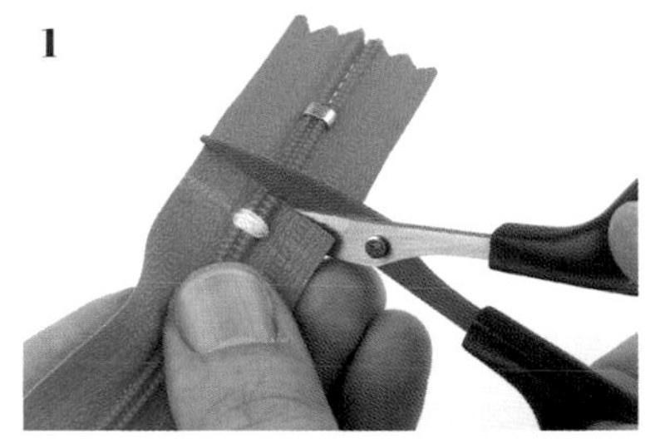

2

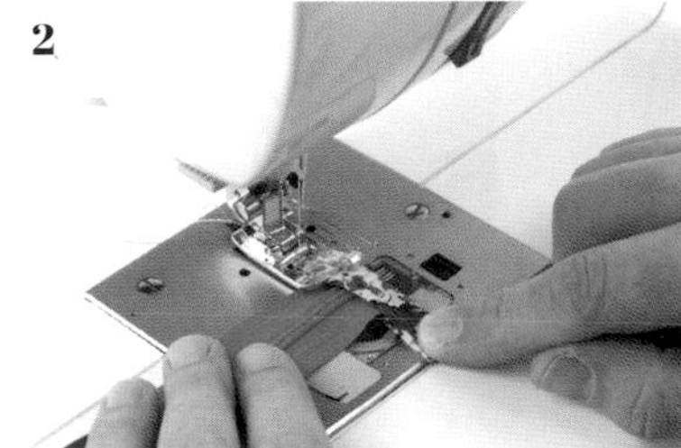

3

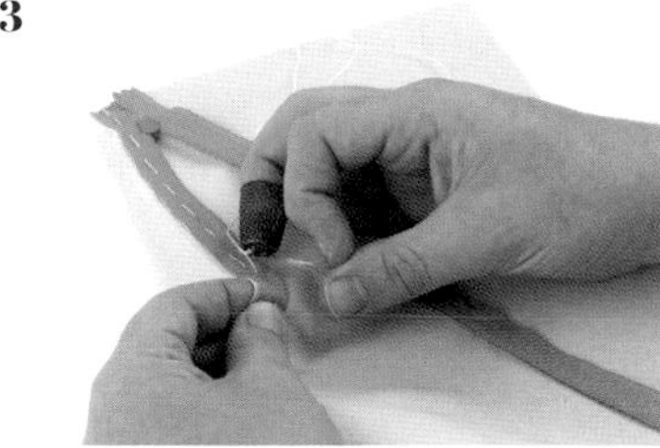

4

5

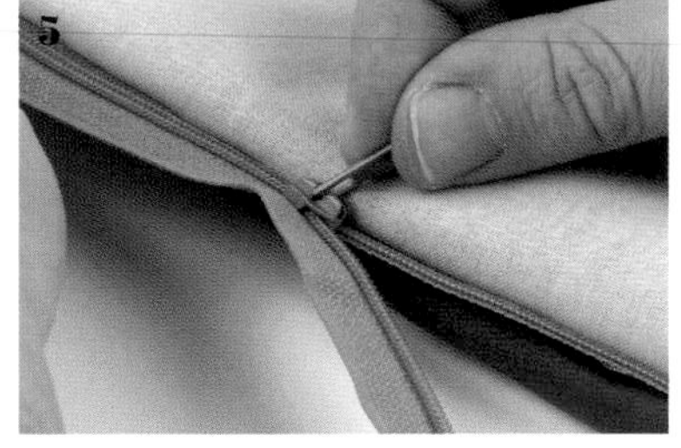

6

1 Measure how long the zip should be. If need be, work some overstitches over the teeth and trim to size.

2 Cut out a small piece of fabric as a tab and topstitch it to the end of the zip, concealing the overstitches.

3 Open the zip and tack/baste one side to the top of your fabric (outer fabric of the project) with the right side of the zip facing down.

4 Now tack/baste the lining section in the same way onto the other side of the zip. The zip will be sandwiched between the two fabrics.

5 Fold both fabrics back on themselves to reveal the zip and test by closing. This will help you see if the zip is in the correct position. Repeat steps 3 and 4 to complete the other side of the zip.

6 Once you are happy with the position of the zip, stitch along the tacking/basting threads (either use a zipper foot, or position the needle to the left – close to the zip – when using the regular foot, as shown). Remove the tacking/basting threads and open out the work to reveal the zip. Press flat.

7

7 Topstitch down each side of the zip to finish.

PIPING WITH AND WITHOUT CORD

Piping may be a doubled strip of fabric sewn into a seam for decoration or it may have a cord enclosed in the fold of the fabric. To make piping with a cord, you need fabric strips cut on the bias, which will fit round the cord well because they are stretchier. You can either cut the bias strips yourself from your chosen fabric (see page 20) or use ready-made bias binding. For the latter, simply iron the folds flat and trim to the desired width.

The seam allowance for sewing in piping is 1cm (½in). A cotton cord about 3mm (⅛in) in diameter requires a bias strip 3cm (1¼in) wide. For thicker cords, cut the strip correspondingly wider.

When sewing in piping it is best to use the zipper foot on your machine, so you can sew as close as possible to the cord. Piping without cord can be sewn in using the normal foot.

1 Fold the strip wrong sides together and insert the cord against the fold. Pin in place and sew along the length of the strip, close to the cord.

2 To fasten the strip to a fabric edge, simply pin in place on the right side with raw edges matching, then sew. If the piping is to go around a curve, clip the strip at approximately 1cm (½in) intervals. This will make it easier to fit it around the curve. Place the second layer of fabric on top, right sides together, and pin. Sew through all layers as close as possible to the cord.

1

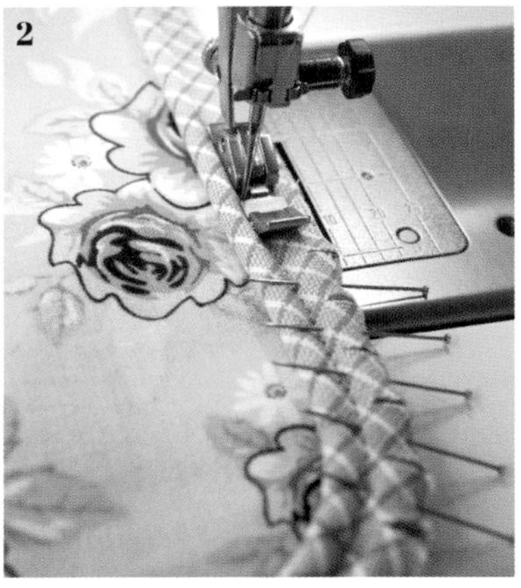
2

MAKING SEWN-IN FRILLS

These frills look great used around the edges of pillows. They are sewn into the seam and look particularly chunky because of the double layer of fabric. To make a frill to go around a pillow, measure the circumference of the pillow and multiply this by two.

1 Cut the strip to twice the desired width plus seam allowances. Fold it in half with the wrong sides together. To sew a gathering stitch along the long open edge, loosen the tension of the upper thread, which will make it easier to pull the lower thread later. Set the stitch length as long as possible (about 5) and sew two rows of parallel stitches close to the outer edge. It is a good idea to use a very strong thread for the lower thread.

2 Gather the frill to the required length by pulling the threads. Knot the threads to keep the gathers in place.

3 Pin the frill to the front of the pillow cover with the right sides together. Sew close to the edge to hold it in place. Place the pillow back on top, right sides together, sew through all the layers, then turn the pillow to the right side.

1

2

The projects

LEVEL OF DIFFICULTY KEY	
I	EASY
II	MEDIUM
III	HARD

SIZE: 16.5 x 24CM (6½ x 9½IN)

LEVEL OF DIFFICULTY

YOU WILL NEED

FABRIC:

- red cotton fabric with white spots, 26 x 50cm (10¼ x 20in)
- about 30 different colourful fabric remnants, each at least 6.5 x 3-9cm (2½ x 1¼-3½in)

WADDING/BATTING:

- fusible, 26 x 40cm (10¼ x 16in)

ADDITIONAL ITEMS:

- 1 white zip, 20cm (8in) long
- template, see page 184; add a 6mm (¼in) seam allowance all round

CUTTING OUT

The following measurements include a 6mm (¼in) seam allowance:

SPOTTED FABRIC:

- 4 strips, 5 x 21.5cm (2 x 8½in), for the top band and its facing
- 2 pouches, using the template on page 184, for the lining

FABRIC REMNANTS:

- approximately 30 rectangles, each 6.5cm (2½in) wide and 3-9cm (1¼-3½in) long
- 4.5 x 31.5cm (1¾ x 12½in) strip for the strap

FUSIBLE WADDING/BATTING:

- 2 strips, 5 x 21.5cm (2 x 8½in)
- 2 pouches, using the template on page 184

Make-up Pouch

1 Sew the remnant rectangles together along the 6.5cm (2½in) edges to form strips about 30cm (12in) long. Sew the strips together along the long edges to make a large rectangle. From this, cut two pouches using the template (see page 184). Now fuse the corresponding wadding/batting to the back of each one. Fuse wadding/batting to the wrong side of two of the spotted strips for the top bands.

2 With right sides facing, sew one wadded top band to the top edge of each wadded pouch piece. Press the seam allowances towards the top band then topstitch in place, close to the seam on the top band.

3 Join each remaining top band (without wadding/batting) to the top of each spotted pouch piece, stitching with right sides facing. Press the seam. These pieces will be the lining.

4 Place the zip flush with the top edge of one wadded pouch piece, on the top band and with right sides facing. Pin a lining on top, right side down, with edges matching, then stitch along the zip edge using the zip foot on your machine. Open out the fabric pieces and fold wrong sides together, matching the raw edges. Topstitch close to the zip teeth on the right side; press carefully. Repeat for the other side of the zip.

5 Make the strap in the same way as for the ties on page 16. Topstitch both of the long edges close to the folds. Fold the strap in half and zigzag the short ends together.

6 Tack/baste the strap ends flush with the side edge of the top band on one wadded pouch piece, with the main part of the strap resting on the right side of the band. Arrange the pouch pieces right sides together, lining against lining and patchwork against patchwork; open the zip. Sew together around the edge, leaving a gap of about 10cm (4in) in the lining section for turning out.

7 Turn the pouch right sides out, pushing the seams out well. Sew up the opening in the lining with small hand stitches and press the bag lightly. Push the lining inside the pouch.

GREENLEAF

SIZE: 30 x 22 x 20CM (12 x 8¾ x 7¾IN)

LEVEL OF DIFFICULTY

YOU WILL NEED

FABRIC:

- piece of denim, 40cm (16in) by the width of the fabric
- scraps of blue, mustard, black and white fabrics, each at least 5cm (2in) square
- fabric for your basket's base, 32.5 x 22.5cm (13 x 9in)
- scrap piece of leather or faux leather, cut to make two handles, each approximately 2 x 30cm (¾ x 12in)

INTERFACING:

- sew-in foam, 60 x 62cm (24 x 24½in)

WADDING/BATTING:

- lightweight soft cotton-mix fleece, about 80 x 86cm (31½ x 34in)

ADDITIONAL ITEMS:

- 4 gold Chicago screws
- hole punch or bradawl

Fabric Basket

1 Begin with a piece of wadding/batting about 40 x 30cm (16 x 12in) and draw a box on it with your marker, measuring 30 x 22cm (12 x 8¾in). This box represents one of the rectangular sides of the basket, and we are going to 'colour it in' with fabric. On one of the long sides of the rectangle, measure down by 5.5cm (2¼in) and mark a line all the way across; this will be the top of the basket. Leave this top rectangle free, as it will be filled with denim in step 4.

2 We are now going to work a form of quilt-as-you-go (see page 23). Choose a scrap piece of fabric – mine is approximately 8 x 18cm (3¼ x 7in). Overlapping your drawn left-hand edge slightly, sew this scrap onto the wadding/batting by channel quilting multiple vertical lines, each about 1cm (⅜in) apart.

3 Now choose two to three smaller fabric scraps and sew them together along the shorter ends to make a piece about the same length as the first fabric piece. Lay this second piece onto the first piece, right sides together, and sew a regular seam to the right-hand side of the first strip to attach it. Flip it over and finger press. Channel quilt over the second piece as you did for the first. Keep going like this, mixing and matching your scraps, and quilting vertically. The most important thing is to ensure that your pieces overlap the lines slightly, as this will ensure there are no gaps. When you have finished 'colouring' the bottom part, redraw the original box lines over the top of the patches. This is helpful for the next step and allows you to see if you have covered everything.

4 Cut a piece of denim slightly larger than the 5.5cm (2¼in) strip you drew in step 1, about 32 x 7cm (12½ x 2¾in) in size, and attach it to the wadding/batting. Using the same method as before, lay the denim piece onto the row of fabric patches and sew with a normal seam. Flip it over and channel quilt, this time horizontally.

5 Make another rectangular side and two ends for the basket, following the instructions in steps 1 to 4: make the second side the same size as the first; the two ends each measure 20 x 22cm (7¾ x 8¾in) so you will have to cut generous pieces of wadding/batting accordingly. You will also need to measure down and mark a 5.5cm (2¼in) line for the denim top on each one.

Tip

Each panel of the basket is made separately and then the basket is constructed side by side in step 8. The trick is to not sew right to the bottom of each panel in order to keep the corners sharp. To do this, simply start sewing as normal at the top of the panel and then stop 6mm (¼in) from the bottom. Mark this point before you start with a water-soluble marker.

6 The base is 20 x 30cm (7¾ x 12in) and uses the 32.5 x 22.5cm (13 x 9in) piece of fabric. Simply lay it over the top of a piece of wadding/batting and then quilt it with your desired pattern – I have swapped to a classic diagonal lattice quilt pattern for my base.

7 Attach the base, side and end panels to pieces of foam interfacing by sewing along the drawn lines. Cut each piece out, leaving a 6mm (¼in) margin outside the sewing line to form a seam allowance.

8 Sew the basket sides and ends right sides together, remembering to stop sewing 6mm (¼in) from the bottom (see tip, left). Sew in the base with the quilted side facing down. This is your basket outer.

9 Make your lining from the denim fabric by cutting panels as follows:

SIDES: 2 pieces, 30 x 22cm (12 x 8¾in)
ENDS: 2 pieces, 20 x 22cm (7¾ x 8¾in)
BASE: 1 piece, 20 x 30cm (7¾ x 12in)

Sew the sides and ends together, remembering to stop sewing 6mm (¼in) from the bottom. Sew in the base, leaving a gap in one long side for turning through.

10 A bit of squashing is required now. With the basket outer the right way out and the basket lining inside out, pull the lining on over the outer (the right sides should be together). Sew around the top edge. Turn the basket out through the gap in the lining and gently pull everything into place. Push the lining into the basket and topstitch the top edge. Close the gap in the lining.

11 Attach a handle to each end of your fabric basket, using your scraps of leather and the Chicago screws. With a hole punch or bradawl make two holes on one basket end, roughly 5cm (2in) from either side. Make two holes in the handle, too. Unscrew the two parts of one Chicago screw and feed it through your punched hole, attaching the handle before screwing it together again. Ensure that your handles are a practical length and that you can use them – mine are about 28cm (11in) long. In the photo you will see that I have actually used the screws back to front – the flat surface is the 'good side'. I prefer the screw side, but it is up to you – there is no Chicago screw police!

Tip

Chicago screws sound exotic but they are easy to find, cheap to buy and actually wonderful for things like this: they are strong and also look really nice.

SIZE: 11 x 11CM (4½ x 4½IN)

LEVEL OF DIFFICULTY

YOU WILL NEED

FABRIC FOR ONE COASTER:

- remnants of large-print cotton fabric approximately 1–6cm (½–2½in) wide and 4–13cm (1¾–5¼in) long
- printed cotton fabric for the backing, 11 x 11cm (4½ x 4½in)

WADDING/BATTING FOR ONE COASTER:

- thin fleece, 15 x 15cm (6 x 6in)

Patchwork Coasters

1 Arrange the fabric remnants on the wadding/batting, pin in place and then sew each one on using a zigzag stitch with matching or coordinating thread. These remnants can be arranged in any way you wish, and can butt up against each other or overlap.

2 Trim the patchwork piece to 11 x 11cm (4½ x 4½in).

3 Place the square of backing fabric and the patchwork piece wrong sides together, and sew the edges together using a zigzag stitch. Make other coasters in the same way.

noodles
duck · apple
snow
cow
fig
cookies
cookies
kitten
chair

SIZE: 27 x 8CM ($10^5/_8$ x 3¼IN) – YOU WILL MAKE IT TO FIT YOUR MUG

LEVEL OF DIFFICULTY

YOU WILL NEED

FABRIC:

- thick beige wool felt for the outer: mine measured 27 x 8cm (10⅝ x 3¼in)
- thin pink wool felt for the lining: mine measured 27 x 8cm (10⅝ x 3¼in)
- felt scraps in three shades of pink for the hearts

ADDITIONAL ITEMS:

- round elastic, 10cm (4in)
- 1 cute button (I used a medium-sized wooden one)
- fabric glue stick
- embroidery hoop for free-motion embroidery (optional)
- heart template, see page 184

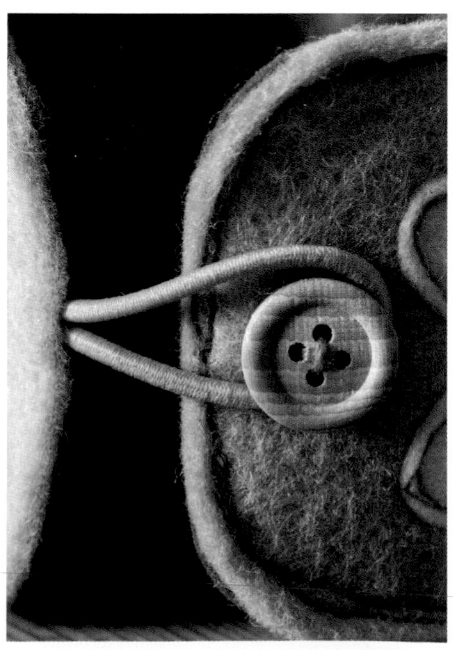

Love Hearts Mug Hug

1 This project has no pattern because you need to custom-fit it to your mug. Measure your mug around the 'waist' – mine is 28cm (11in) in circumference. Subtract 1cm (⅜in) from this. Now measure the height – mine is 10cm (4in). Subtract 2cm (¾in). Therefore, the size I need to cut my felt pieces to is 27 x 8cm (10⅝ x 3¼in). Cut two felt panels to this size, one from thick felt, one from thin felt. Use a round item, such as your mug, to round off the corners of both pieces.

2 Using the heart template on page 184, cut out six hearts – two from each colour – from your selection of pink felt scraps. Position the hearts along the middle of the thick felt panel with their tails pointing towards the centre. Glue them in place.

3 Set your machine up for free-motion embroidery (see page 19) and embroider the hearts with the coordinating thread.

4 Lightly glue the embroidered outer to the lining piece. Fold the elastic in half to make a loop and tuck the ends in between the lining and outer pieces at one short end.

5 Free-motion embroider around the outside of the mug hug to attach the felt pieces together, and to secure the elastic loop. Trim all threads away. Sew the button onto the short end of the mug hug on the opposite side to the loop. Put the kettle on!

SIZE: 11 x 13CM (4½ x 5IN)

LEVEL OF DIFFICULTY

YOU WILL NEED

FABRIC:

- floral cotton, 37 x 16cm (14½ x 6¼in)

EMBELLISHMENTS:

- small pieces of lace, rickrack and ribbon, long enough to fit across the heart
- satin ribbon, 28cm (11in) long
- three or more wooden buttons

ADDITIONAL ITEMS:

- toy stuffing
- heart template, see page 185

Floral Heart

1 Fold the floral fabric in half, right sides together. Pin on the heart template and cut out.

2 Take one heart and arrange the pieces of ribbon, lace and rickrack across the shape at different angles. Pin in place and sew with matching thread.

3 Pin the two heart pieces together, right sides facing, and sew around the shape taking a 1cm (½in) seam allowance, leaving a gap for turning through and back-tacking at the beginning and end of the stitch line.

4 Clip the curves and point of the heart and turn through. Roll the seams gently to improve the shape then stuff the heart with small pieces of stuffing. Hand-sew the opening closed.

5 Sew on a button (or buttons) as decoration. Position the ribbon for the hanging loop, following the photograph opposite for guidance, and sew it in place with small stitches. Place buttons over the top of the stitches and sew in place. Trim the ends of the ribbon to neat points.

2

SIZE: 5 x 18.5CM (2 x 7¼IN)

LEVEL OF DIFFICULTY ⌶⌶

YOU WILL NEED

FABRIC:

- outer cotton, 20 x 27cm (8 x 10¾in)
- lining cotton, 20 x 27cm (8 x 10¾in)

WADDING/BATTING:

- thick, fluffy fleece, 20 x 27cm (8 x 10¾in)

ADDITIONAL ITEMS:

- 1 red zip, 20cm (8in)
- satin ribbon, 20cm (8in)
- 2 wooden beads in red and pink
- template, see page 187, includes a 6mm (¼in) seam allowance

CUTTING OUT

- Cut the template from outer, lining and wadding/batting

Pencil Case

1 Place the outer fabric pencil-case piece on top of the wadding/batting and sew the long edges together using zigzag stitch.

2 Fold the lining along the fabric fold and then cut it, to create two identical pieces.

3 With the right sides facing, position the zip flush against one long edge of the outer fabric (the underside of the zip should be facing up and the zip pull on the left). Then place one of the lining pieces on top, right side facing down, aligning all the raw edges. Pin in place. Using the zipper foot, sew along the zip.

4 Open out the fabrics and, with the right sides facing, sandwich the free side of the zip between the opposite long edge of the outer fabric and the remaining lining piece, right sides facing.

5 With the right sides facing, neatly sew the side edges of the outer case together. Sew each outer bottom corner to make a boxed base (see page 16). Open the zip.

6 Sew the sides and bottom of the lining together in the same way, leaving a turning gap of about 7cm (2¾in) in the bottom. Turn the pencil case right side out and carefully shape the corners of the outer fabric and lining. Fold the seam allowance of the turning gap to the inside, and sew up on the machine. Push the lining inside.

7 Thread the satin ribbon through the hole in the zip pull. Grasp the two ends of the ribbon and thread them through the wooden beads. Knot to secure.

SIZE: 11 x 11CM (4½ x 4½IN)

LEVEL OF DIFFICULTY

YOU WILL NEED

FABRIC:

- light blue wool felt, 12.5 x 25cm (5 x 10in)
- white wool felt, 12.5 x 25cm (5 x 10in)
- yellow wool felt, 5 x 5cm (2 x 2in)

FILLING:

- polyester stuffing, or see tip (below right)

ADDITIONAL ITEMS:

- fabric glue stick
- templates, see page 185

Daisy Pincushion

1 Cut two daisies from white felt and one centre from yellow felt, using the templates (see page 185).

2 Cut the blue felt into two 12.5cm (5in) squares. Take one square of blue felt and glue your first daisy on, centrally.

3 Using white thread, attach the flower by stitching a line down the middle of each petal. Lay the second daisy on top, offsetting the petals and again sewing down the middle of each petal. Leave the daisy petals loose on both sides of the sewing line for a 3D effect.

4 Swap to a yellow thread and sew the daisy centre in place.

5 Place the other blue felt square right sides together on top. Sew around the perimeter, leaving a gap for turning out. Cut across the corners to reduce bulk and turn out through the gap. Fill the pincushion well with stuffing and sew the gap closed by hand.

Tip

If you fill your pincushion with un-soaped, fine steel wool it will sharpen your pins every time you push them in or pull them out, keeping them sharp and ready for use.

SIZE: 33CM (13IN) HIGH

LEVEL OF DIFFICULTY

YOU WILL NEED

FABRIC:

- 7 different batik fabrics in a range of blues, purples and greens, about 15cm (6in) wide by 110cm (44in) long
- batik fabric for the lining, 55 x 80cm (21¾ x 31½in)
- scraps of colourful fabric for the rosettes

WADDING/BATTING:

- sew-in, 50 x 100cm (19¾ x 39½in)

ADDITIONAL ITEMS:

- 1 karabiner (swivel key holder)
- 1 sew-on magnetic press-stud
- coordinating decorative buttons

CUTTING OUT

HANDLES:

- Cut 2 strips from a patchwork of main fabrics, each 12 x 50cm (4¾ x 19¾in).

The following measurements include a 6mm (¼in) seam allowance:

ASSORTED BATIK FABRICS:

- strips, 80cm (31½in) long in different widths

LINING FABRIC:

- 50 x 80cm (19¾ x 31½in), for the bag lining
- 1 strip 4 x 25cm (1½ x 10in), for a key loop

WADDING/BATTING:

- 50 x 80cm (19¾ x 31½in) rectangle
- 2 strips 4 x 50cm (1½ x 19¾in), for the handles

Sea Breeze Tote Bag

1 Lay the wadding/batting rectangle on the work surface. Lay the first strip of batik fabric right side up on top, matching one 80cm (31½in) edge. Lay the second strip of fabric on top of the first, right sides together, and sew through all the layers using the width of the presser foot as a guide for the seam allowance.

2 Fold back the top strip of fabric and press, so that the right side of the fabric is visible. Repeat this process of covering, stitching and folding back, until the whole of the wadding/batting rectangle is covered with strips of fabric (see page 23). To prevent the rectangle from becoming distorted, alternate the sewing direction, i.e. sew from the top down then from the bottom up.

3 Fold the rectangle in half, right sides together, so that it measures 40 x 50cm (15¾ x 19¾in), then sew up the side seams.

4 Iron the bag, pressing along the bottom fold to mark the centre of the base. At one corner, fold the side seam over the bottom crease and sew to create a box base (see page 16); stitch across the triangle 10cm (4in) away from the point. Trim off the excess fabric to leave a small seam allowance and zigzag the edges together. Repeat on the other side to shape the bag base.

5 Sew together the lining as for the outer bag, leaving a gap in a side seam for turning out. Shape the base as before.

Continued overleaf...

6 Press 1cm (⅜in) to the wrong side along one long edge of each handle strip. Lay a strip of wadding/batting centrally over the wrong side of the strip. First fold the unfinished long edge over onto the wadding/batting and then fold the ironed long edge over the top, so that the fabric edges overlap. Topstitch close to the folded edge through all the layers. Work a second line of topstitching an even distance away to secure the layers further and for decoration.

7 Fold the key-loop strip in half lengthways, right sides together, and sew the long edges together. Turn the strip right sides out. Arrange the long seam so that it is in the centre and press. Fold the strip so the ends meet with the long seam hidden in the middle. Slip the karabiner hook onto the loop.

Tip

If you want to make inside pockets from the fabric remnants, they must be sewn to the right side of the lining before the lining is secured to the bag.

8 With the outer bag inside out, place the lining into the bag, right sides together. Slip the ends of the handles between the layers of fabric so that the raw edges are level and the main part of each handle is between the fabric layers – one on each side of the bag, with the ends of the handles about 12cm (4¾in) away from the side seams. Insert the key loop in the same way, between one of the handles and the side seam. Sew around the top edge of the bag and then turn the bag out through the opening in the lining. Close the opening with small hand stitches and then push the lining into the bag. Topstitch the top of the bag 1cm (⅜in) from the edge.

9 For the button rosettes, cut several circles with different diameters from the remnants of fabric. Roll a small hem to the wrong side of each circle and work running stitch along the turned fabric using a matching double thread (see page 158). Pull up the thread to gather the fabric then flatten the fabric into a circle and even out the folds. Tie off the thread ends and use them to sew the rosette, together with a decorative button, to the bag.

10 Sew the two sections of the magnetic press-stud inside the bag at the centres of the top edges to close it.

Tip

To cut the circles for the rosettes, use a round plastic template or draw around a glass or other round object.

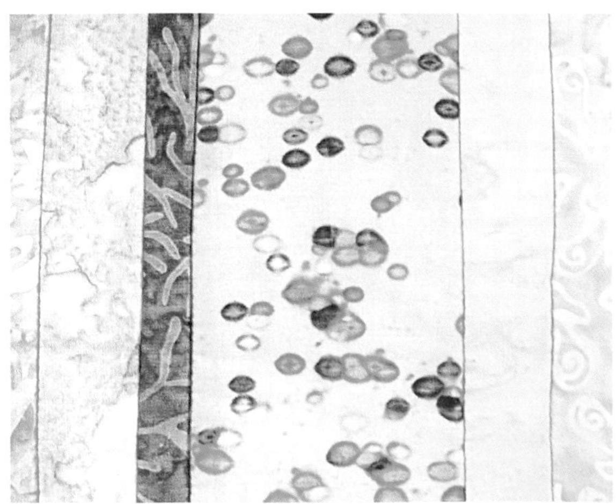

SIZE: 12 x 15CM (4¾ x 6IN)

LEVEL OF DIFFICULTY

YOU WILL NEED

FABRIC:

- A: patterned blue cotton (outer), 50 x 60cm (19¾ x 23½in)
- B: patterned light green cotton (compartments), 25 x 40cm (9¾ x 15¾in)
- C: plain blue cotton (lining), 35 x 20cm (13¾ x 7¾in)
- D: turquoise cotton with white dots (lining zip compartment), 25 x 20cm (9¾ x 7¾in)

WADDING/BATTING:

- medium-weight, iron-on fleece, 35 x 20cm (13¾ x 7¾in)

INTERFACING:

- firm iron-on, 25 x 30cm (9¾ x 11¾in)

ADDITIONAL ITEMS:

- 1 blue zip, 15cm (6in)
- bias binding in spotty turquoise, 18mm (¾in) wide, 16cm (6¼in) long
- 1 twist purse closure, 3.5 x 2cm (1⅜x ¾in)
- carpet knife or small scissors

CUTTING OUT

The following measurements include a 6mm (¼in) seam allowance:

- From fabric A: 1 piece, 30.5 x 16.5cm (12 x 6½in) and 3 pieces, 22 x 16.5cm (8¾ x 6½in)
- From fabric B: 2 pieces, 22 x 16.5cm (8¾ x 6½in)
- From fabric C: 1 piece, 30.5 x 16.5cm (12 x 6½in)
- From fabric D: 1 piece, 22 x 16.5cm (8¾ x 6½in)
- 30.5 x 16.5cm (12 x 6½in) fleece
- 30.5 x 16.5cm (12 x 6½in) interfacing

The Perfect Purse

1 For the card compartments, fold two 22 x 16.5cm (8¾ x 6½in) pieces of fabric A and the two 22 x 16.5cm (8¾ x 6½in) pieces of fabric B in half widthways, wrong sides together, and edge stitch along the folds.

2 Place one folded piece of fabric B on the table, and put one folded piece of fabric A on top, 7mm (¼in) from the top (edge-stitched) edge. Place a credit card between the two layers. Mark the bottom edge of the card with a pin, and sew the fabric layers together about 2mm (⅛in) below this mark. Then sew together the second set of folded fabrics in the same way. Pin the two sets of fabric together, so that all the folded edges sit 7mm (¼in) apart.

3 Fold the bias binding in half and hold against the last seam. Determine where to cut the bottom edges of the compartments so that the seam is just covered. Cut the bottom edges accordingly.

4 Next, sew the central seam of the pocket compartment from bottom to top. Then sew the seams to the left and right: put a credit card in the top compartment and run a fingernail down its edge. Sew slightly outside this line. Repeat on the other side. Sew the bias binding to the bottom edge of the compartments.

5 For the zip compartment, with the right sides facing, position the zip flush against the top (short) edge of the remaining 22 x 16.5cm (8¾ x 6½in) piece of fabric A (so the underside of the zip should be facing up and the zip pull on the left). About 1cm (⅜in) of the metal end piece of the zip should be on the fabric. Place your fabric D piece on top, with the right sides facing, and pin, sandwiching the zip. Sew the edge together with a zipper foot, then open out and press. Edge stitch just below the zip.

Continued overleaf...

6 Now manipulate the zip fabrics to trap the other side of the zip between them, right sides facing. Pin and then sew together. Open the zip all the way. Turn right side out, pull tight, and topstitch the second edge (this is a little fiddly). Press flat with the zip about 2cm (¾in) from the top edge.

7 Iron fabric C to the adhesive side of the fleece. Now sew on the various parts of the interior: place the zip compartment flush against the short bottom edge of the fabric, right sides facing up, and edge stitch together. Then sew across the top edge of the zipped compartment.

8 Place the credit card compartment 1.5cm (½in) above the zip compartment, right sides facing up, then sew along the bias binding to secure.

9 Iron the interfacing onto the wrong side of the remaining piece of fabric A. Place this interfaced piece right sides together with your purse interior and sew all round, leaving a turning gap of about 10cm (4in) in the bottom. Trim the corner seam allowances at an angle and carefully turn the purse right side out. Press. Turn the seam allowance of the turning opening to the inside and pin. Edge stitch the flap section (the top of the purse) and the bottom edge of the purse to close the turning gap.

10 To attach the purse closure, mark the middle of the flap 1.5cm (½in) from the top. Put the locking part for the flap in the middle, and draw on the central oval. Use scissors to cut the fabric within the oval without getting too close to the drawn edge. Attach the closure in accordance with the manufacturer's instructions, and neaten the area around the oval. This is a little tricky to do, and is easiest done with scissors or a carpet knife.

11 Position the bottom part of the closure (the turning part) on the folded piece of the purse so that it is easy to close. Push the sharp points of the closure lightly onto the fabric, and cut the indentations with a carpet knife. Be sure to open the change compartment first and insert something as protection to prevent damage to the other fabric pieces. Now pierce the sharp points through the fabric and push to the outside to finish your purse.

SIZE: 28.5 x 19.5CM (11¼ x 7¾IN)

LEVEL OF DIFFICULTY

YOU WILL NEED

FABRIC:

- light brown cotton, 15 x 60cm (6 x 24in)
- geometric cotton, 5 x 60cm (2 x 24in)
- spot cotton, 30 x 49cm (12 x 19½in)

WADDING/BATTING:

- 30 x 21cm (12 x 8¼in)

If you want to make a matching mug cosy, see opposite for more information.

CUTTING OUT

The following measurements include a 6mm (¼in) seam allowance:

- 5 x 60cm (2 x 23½in) light brown fabric for the checkerboard pattern
- 5 x 60cm (2 x 23½in) geometric fabric for the checkerboard pattern
- 10 x 19cm (4 x 7½in) light brown fabric for the spoon pocket background
- 10 x 20cm (4 x 8in) light brown fabric for spoon pocket
- 3 pieces spotted fabric, 4 x 19cm (1½ x 7½in), for the vertical borders
- 2 pieces spotted fabric for the top and bottom edging, 4 x 30cm (1½ x 12in)
- 30 x 21cm (12 x 8¼in) spotted fabric for the back
- 30 x 21cm (12 x 8¼in) wadding/batting

Pocket Mug Rug

1 Join the two 5cm (2in) strips for the checkerboard pattern along one long edge (figure 1). Press the seam open. Cut this strip into ten sections 5cm (2in) wide (figure 2). Sew two sections together to make a row (figure 3). Sew a total of five rows. Join the rows together, rotating alternate rows by 180 degrees (figure 4).

2 Attach a 4 x 19cm (1½ x 7½in) strip of spotted fabric to the left and right sides of the checkerboard.

3 Fold the pocket fabric in half widthways with wrong sides facing along the longer edge. Tack/baste the folded pocket to the pocket background, matching three edges but not the folded top edge. Sew the pocket to the strip on the right of the checkerboard and then attach the remaining 4 x 19cm (1½ x 7½in) strip to the other side of the pocket.

4 Attach the two edging strips to the top and bottom edges to complete the front of the mug rug.

5 Place the front on the back piece, right sides together, and then pin the wadding/batting on top. Stitch together all round, leaving a small gap along one long edge for turning. Trim the seam allowances at the corners and turn right side out. Tuck in the seam allowances at the opening and close with small hand-stitches. Stitch in the ditch (sew along the seam lines) to quilt the layers together.

Figure 1

Figure 2

Figure 3

Figure 4

Design by Kerstin Porsch

MUG COSY

- Measure the height and circumference of the mug. Cut a rectangle to this dimension from light brown fabric, patterned fabric and wadding/batting. You will also need 2 tie strips, 5 x 50cm (2 x 19¾in).
- Pin the two fabric rectangles right sides together with the wadding/batting on top and stitch all round, leaving a gap for turning. Turn out, trim and finish as for the mug rug.
- Fold each tie strip in half lengthways, right sides together, then sew the long sides together and turn out. Pin centrally on the rectangle with one above and one below the mug handle. Topstitch in place along the long edges. Knot the ends.

Sakura Box Bag

SIZE: 22 x 12 x 12CM (8¾ x 4¾ x 4¾IN)

LEVEL OF DIFFICULTY

YOU WILL NEED

FABRIC:

- red and white spotted cotton outer fabric, 70 x 25cm (27½ x 10in)
- floral cotton fabric for the appliqué, 10 x 10cm (4 x 4in)
- natural-coloured linen for the lining, 60 x 20cm (24 x 8in)

WADDING/BATTING:

- lightweight, fusible fleece, 60 x 20cm (24 x 8in)

ADDITIONAL ITEMS:

- 1 zip, 30cm (12in)
- double-sided iron-on fusible webbing, 10 x 10cm (4 x 4in)
- templates, see page 186

CUTTING OUT

When cutting out template A, add 6mm (¼in) seam allowance on all sides. All other dimensions include a 6mm (¼in) seam allowance.

- 2 pieces of red and white spotted cotton using template A
- 1 piece of red and white spotted cotton 8 x 22cm (3¼ x 8¾in) for the loop
- 1 piece of floral fabric 10 x 10cm (4 x 4in) for the appliqué
- 2 pieces of wadding/batting using template A
- 2 pieces of linen using template A

1 For the outer, iron the corresponding wadding/batting pieces onto the backs of both cut-out pieces of red and white spotted cotton fabric.

2 Place the floral fabric piece onto the iron-on fusible webbing and iron together. Using template B, cut the cherry blossom motif out carefully. Pull off the backing paper when done.

3 Place the cherry blossom motif onto one of the red and white spotted bag pieces and iron on. Sew around the edges using satin stitch (stitch length 0.5mm; stitch width 2mm).

4 Position the zip along the top edge of the appliqué piece, right sides facing, then top with a linen bag piece, right side down. Secure and stitch together along the edge of the zip.

5 Fold the pieces over so that the wrong sides are now facing. Iron, then edgestitch along the zip seam. Repeat for the other side of the zip.

6 Sew each outer piece to its corresponding lining piece, wrong sides together, using a zigzag stitch within the seam allowance. Treat each pair as one piece from now on.

7 Make the strip for the loop as described on page 16 and sew the ends onto the end of the zip seam (the loop should be on the zip and pointing to the inside). Half open the zip. Sew the lower edges together, right sides facing. Close the side seams (a1 + a2), then the side seams (b1 + b2).

8 Turn the bag right sides out through the zip opening.

SIZE: 25CM (10IN) DIAMETER

LEVEL OF DIFFICULTY

YOU WILL NEED

FABRIC:

- pale fabric, 37cm (14½in) square
- scraps of wool felt in blue and green
- purple felt for the back, 37cm (14½in) square

WADDING/BATTING:

- lightweight, fusible fleece, 37cm (14½in) square

ADDITIONAL ITEMS:

- purple perle no. 8 cotton
- embroidery thread/floss
- embroidery hoop, 25cm (10in) in diameter
- fabric glue stick
- hot-glue gun and glue
- templates, see page 187
- interfacing or fabric offcuts to fill the back of the hoop
- water-soluble marker pen

Hoop Art

1 Fuse the wadding/batting to the wrong side of the pale fabric. Take apart your embroidery hoop, place the smaller ring onto the fabric and draw around it with the water-soluble marker. This gives you your working area.

2 Using the template, cut out the main bird shape from the green felt and its wing from the blue felt. Find the centre of the circle on the fabric and glue on both the green bird and blue wing with the glue stick. Mark the border and the three crest feathers on the bird's head with your water-soluble marker.

3 Referring to the embroidery stitches on page 17, embroider the edge of the bird's body with a running stitch and its wing with chain stitch, using the perle cotton. Use backstitch and French knots to create the three feathers. Work a French knot once more for the bird's eye. Finally, backstitch the border. Note: for this outer embellishment, go just over the edge of the drawn circle if you would like the ends to be hidden when the hoop is assembled.

4 Fit the embroidery into the hoop and tighten the screw. Lightly mist the front with clean water to remove the marker lines (this will slightly shrink and tighten the embroidery in the hoop too).

5 Trim back the excess fabric so that there is about 3.5cm (1⅜in) overhang all around. Hot glue this to the underside of the back of the hoop to keep it out of the way. Use some interfacing offcuts to stuff the back of the hoop so that things stay nice and taut and don't sag. Hot glue the large purple felt piece to the back of your hoop then trim away the excess to create a neat, rounded edge.

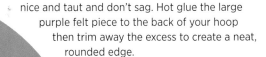

SIZE: 12CM (4¾IN) HIGH

LEVEL OF DIFFICULTY

YOU WILL NEED

FABRIC:

- floral turquoise cotton, 34 x 26cm (13½ x 10¼in)
- turquoise patterned cotton, 20 x 22.5cm (8 x 9in)
- scrap of red patterned cotton

WADDING/BATTING:

- iron-on fleece, 24.5 x 34cm (10 x 13½in)

ADDITIONAL ITEMS:

- scraps of synthetic stuffing
- fabric glue
- strong sewing thread
- 1 can, 12cm (4¾in) tall and 32cm (12½in) in circumference (open the can you are going to cover with a can opener that won't leave sharp edges)

Fabric Caddy

COVER FOR THE TIN

1 Fold the turquoise flowered fabric in half lengthways, wrong sides together, and press – this crease serves as a marker for the upper edge. Cut a piece of wadding/batting to 34 x 12cm (13½ x 4¾in). Open up the fabric and fuse the wadding/batting to one half, positioning the wadding/batting a little way from the crease so there is no wadding/batting on the seam allowance.

2 Fold the fabric in half, right sides together (so the wadding/batting is on the outside), and sew along the long open edge to form a tube. Turn the tube the right way out and iron. Neaten the short edges with zigzag stitch.

3 Fold the tube in half crossways, right sides together, and sew the short edges together. Iron open the seam allowance. Turn through, then slip the tube over the can.

FABRIC LID

1 For the underside of the lid, draw twice around the can lid on the turquoise patterned fabric and cut out without adding a seam allowance. Cut a slit in one of the pieces for turning through. Place the circles right sides together, and place both on a piece of wadding/batting. Sew all around through all layers. Trim the wadding/batting close to the seam and clip the fabric close to the stitching. Turn through and press.

2 Draw around the can lid on the wadding/batting. Cut out, then glue the piece to the top of the lid; trim away close to the edge.

3 For the upper side of the lid, draw around the can lid on the patterned fabric. Draw a 2.5cm (1in) seam allowance all around, then cut out. Cut another circle of wadding/batting the same size.

4 Sew round the edge of the circle of wadding/batting with strong thread and a long running stitch, starting with a knot and a backstitch. When you have gone full circle, place the can lid in the centre and pull the thread gently to gather the wadding/batting around it. Pull the thread tight and sew in the end. Follow the same procedure with the circle of fabric, then stitch to secure.

5 Sew the smaller fabric circle to the underside by hand, with the opening for turning hidden on the inside.

6 For the bobble, cut a circle of red fabric 7–8cm (2¾–3¼in) in diameter. Gather around the edge, pull the thread a little, then stuff with filling. Pull the thread tight and stitch to the middle of the lid.

EUROPEAN • JAPAN • OLFA PATENTED • U.S.A.

Cutlery Roll

SIZE: 40 x 70CM (15¾ x 27½IN), OPEN WITHOUT TIES

LEVEL OF DIFFICULTY

YOU WILL NEED

FABRIC:

- blue striped cotton for the inner and outer, 2 rectangles, 40 x 72cm (15¾ x 28¼in)
- 12 different cotton strips in blue checks/stripes for the cutlery insert, each 20 x 5.5cm (7¾ x 2¼in)
- dark blue striped cotton for the insert lining, 23 x 50cm (9 x 19¾in)
- 2 different cotton strips in blue checks/stripes for the ties, each 5 x 80cm (2 x 31½in)

WADDING/BATTING:

- thin iron-on fleece, 20 x 50cm (7¾ x 19¾in)
- thick iron-on fleece, 40 x 72cm (15¾ x 28¼in)

ADDITIONAL ITEMS:

- ruler and rotary cutter
- erasable fabric marker pen
- bias tape maker, 25mm (1in) (optional)

1 To make the cutlery insert, sew the long sides of the 12 rectangles together to form a strip. Iron all the seam allowances in one direction. Iron the thin fleece onto the wrong side and trim the overlaps. Straighten the top edge at 90 degrees to the seams, using a ruler and rotary cutter.

2 Place the patchworked strip and the dark blue lining piece right sides together and sew the top edges together. Iron the seam allowance towards the lining. Still with the right sides facing, shift the fabrics so that 1cm (½in) of the lining fabric sits above the patchworked panel, then pin to secure. This gives you a faux binding along the top edge. Trim the insert to 17cm (6¾in) high (or to suit your own cutlery), then sew the sides and bottom edges together, leaving a turning opening in the bottom. Trim the seam allowances at an angle at the corners. Turn the cutlery insert right side out, shaping the corners well, then press and sew up the opening by hand. Topstitch the lining that is visible on the front on the right side.

Continued overleaf...

1

2

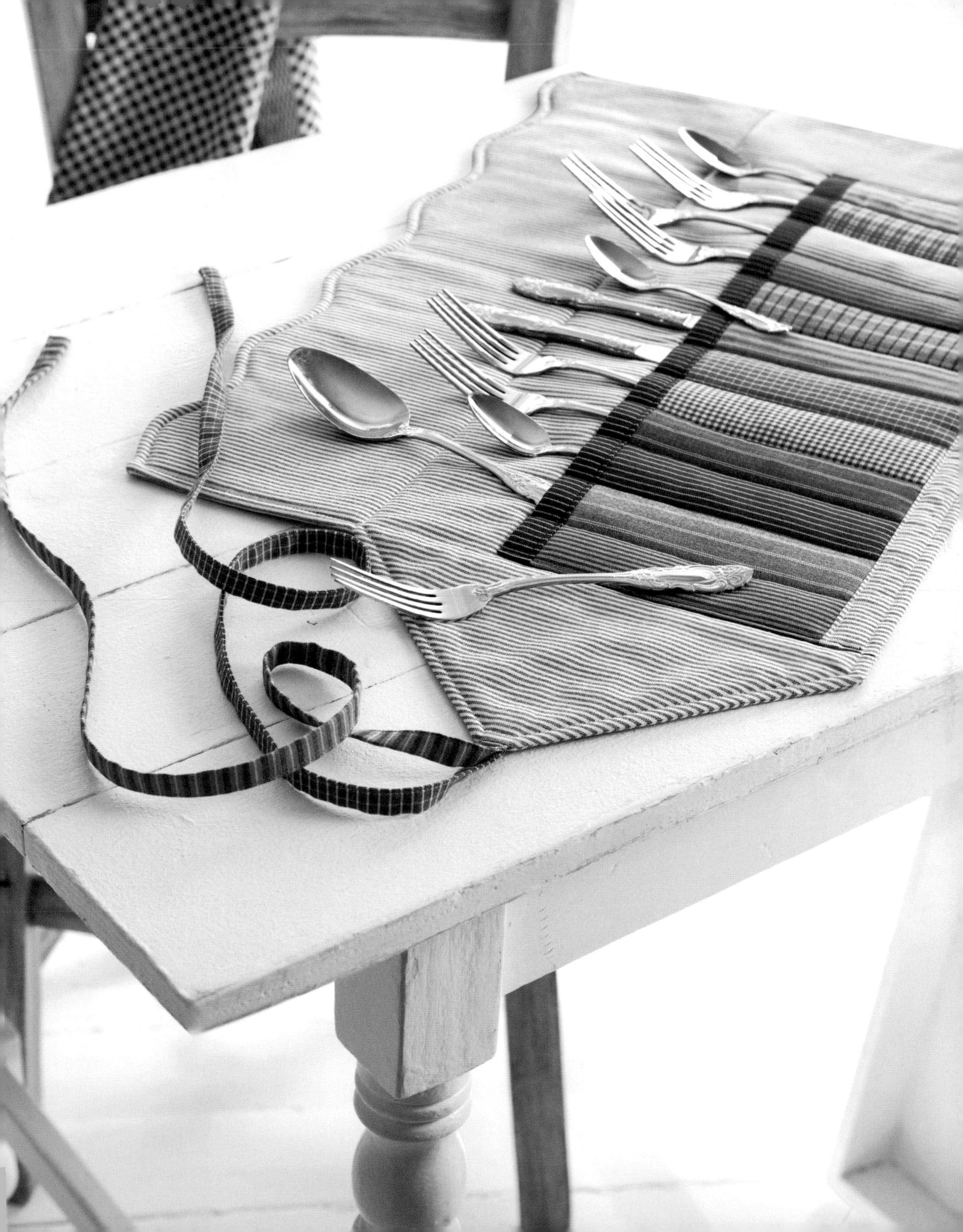

3 For the ties, fold the strips in half lengthwise with the wrong sides facing. Press the folds, then open out and fold one short edge 6mm (¼in) to the inside. Press the long sides to the middle and fold the ties in half lengthwise again. The raw edges will now be on the inside. Alternatively, use a bias tape maker. Edge stitch the open edges together.

4 For the main section, iron your thick fleece onto the wrong side of your inner fabric and trim the overlaps. Transfer the outer sewing lines to the fleece as indicated in the diagram (the black dashed lines). Place the inner and outer rectangles together with the right sides facing and pin within the drawn sewing lines. Push the two ties between the layers and secure the unfinished edges to the tip of the flap (the point of the triangular section). Pin the ties safely to the inside so they can't get caught up in your stitching.

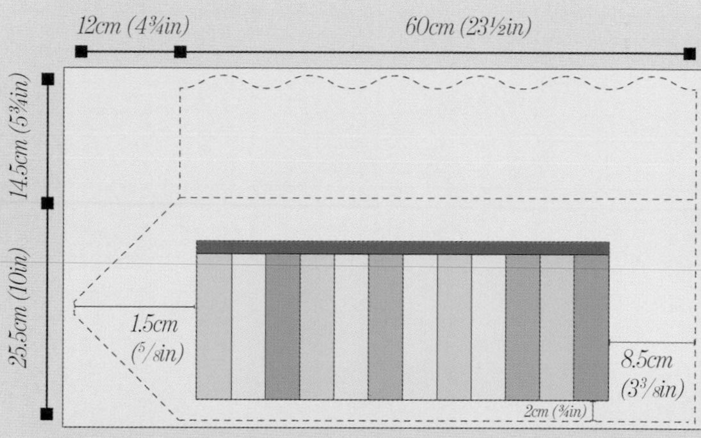

5 Sew all the layers together along the drawn line, leaving a 15cm (6in) turning opening in the bottom edge. Be very careful when working along the wavy line and back-tack at the beginning and end of the seam (at the turning opening). Trim the item 8mm (⅜in) from the seams. Trim the corner seam allowances at an angle and cut tiny triangles out on the inner corner and along the wavy seam, close to the stitching. Turn the roll right side out. Shape the corners and wavy edge well, and sew up the turning opening by hand.

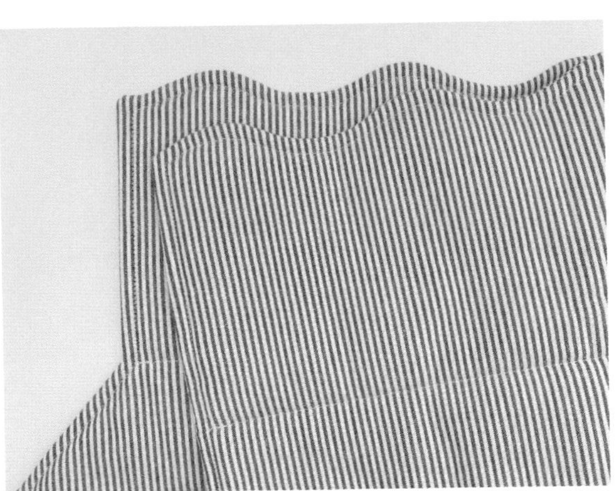

6 Sew all around the cutlery roll, about 8mm (⅜in) from the outer edge. To make the wavy seam particularly successful, it's a good idea to draw the stitch line first with a self-erasing marker pen. To help the fabric fold over the cutlery, draw in the line (red dashed), as indicated on the diagram, opposite. Pin the layers together and sew along the line.

7 Secure the cutlery insert to the lining of the roll. It should be 2cm (¾in) from the bottom edge and 8.5cm (3½in) from the right-hand side. Sew the sections of the cutlery insert by stitching along the seams. Finally, sew the side edges and the bottom edge of the insert.

SIZE: 31 x 25CM (12¼ x 10IN)

LEVEL OF DIFFICULTY

YOU WILL NEED

FABRIC:

- plain fabric for the cosy outer, 26 x 66cm (10¼ x 26in)
- pretty grey-blue fabric for the lining, loop handle and allium flower heads, 33 x 66cm (13 x 26in)

WADDING/BATTING:

- lightweight, fusible fleece, 26 x 66cm (10¼ x 26in)

ADDITIONAL ITEMS:

- water-soluble fabric marker pen
- faux gold leather bias binding (optional)
- coordinating threads for topstitching
- fabric glue stick
- embroidery hoop for FME (optional)
- template, see page 188

Allium Tea Cosy

1 Use the template on page 188 to cut two outer pieces and two lining pieces. Interface the wrong sides of the outer pieces with the wadding/batting and trim.

2 Using the templates, cut three allium head shapes from the lining fabric. You don't need to do this neatly, as they should have a very free-form appearance.

3 Stick them onto one of the outer panels with the fabric glue stick, allowing room for the stems of your flowers – the lowest allium head on mine is about 8cm (3¼in) from the bottom edge. When dry, use the water-soluble marker to draw in the flower details.

4 Using grey thread and free-machine embroidery, embroider over the flower details. Trim away the thread tails. Mist with water to remove the marker lines.

5 Make the top loop handle by cutting a piece of lining fabric 20 x 4cm (8 x 1½in) in size. Fold it in half lengthways and press. Open out and then fold the raw edges to the centre fold and press. Fold in half again and topstitch along both long edges with coordinating thread. Trim the ends of the loop handle then fold it in half to make a loop. Attach to the top of one of the outer panels.

6 I have also added a little gold tag on the side, which is optional. This is just faux leather bias binding and you can find it readily online and in good haberdashers. About 5cm (2in) folded over does the trick. Attach to one of the sides of the outer panels.

7 With the right sides facing, sew the curve of the outer pieces together. Sew the lining pieces together in the same way, but leave a turning gap somewhere. With the outer the right way out and the lining inside out, pull the lining on over the outer and sew around the bottom edge.

8 Turn the tea cosy out through the gap and close it with small hand stitches. Stuff the lining into the outer, but leave a small amount protruding at the bottom (the aim is to make it look like bias binding). Topstitch around the bottom, right on the edge of the 'trim' to keep it in place.

9 Gravity being gravity, your lining will not stay in the tea cosy when it is upside down! A few stitches along the seam line between both layers will keep the lining up where it should be.

SIZE: 73 x 54CM (28¾ x 21¼IN), WITHOUT LOOPS

LEVEL OF DIFFICULTY

Wall Tidy

YOU WILL NEED

FABRIC:

- A: pink patterned cotton, 55 x 110cm (21¾ x 43¼in)
- B: blue patterned cotton, 30 x 65cm (11¾ x 25½in)
- C: light green patterned cotton, 80 x 110cm (31½ x 43¼in)
- D: pink cotton, 45 x 110cm (17¾ x 43¼in)
- E: orange cotton, 10 x 70cm (4 x 27½in)
- F: light green cotton, 10 x 70cm (4 x 27½in)

WADDING/BATTING:

- thick iron-on volume fleece, 60 x 80cm (23½ x 31½in)
- iron-on leather-like interfacing, 60 x 80cm (23½ x 31½in)

CUTTING OUT

Dimensions include an 8mm (³⁄₈in) seam allowance:

- A: 3 strips a of 8 x 110cm (3¼ x 43¼in) (border), 2 squares b of 14.5 x 14.5cm (5¾ x 5¾in) (back of pocket), 2 rectangles c of 26.5 x 14.5cm (10½ x 5¾in) (pocket)
- B: 2 squares b of 14.5 x 14.5cm (5¾ x 5¾in) (back of pocket), 2 rectangles c of 26.5 x 14.5cm (10½ x 5¾in) (pocket)
- C: 2 squares b of 14.5 x 14.5cm (5¾ x 5¾in) (back of pocket), 2 rectangles c of 26.5 x 14.5cm (10½ x 5¾in) (pocket), 1 rectangle d of 75 x 56cm (29½ x 22in) (back of wall tidy)
- D: 2 strips e of 8 x 60cm (3¼ x 23½in) (edging right/left), 2 strips f of 8 x 53.5cm (3¼ x 21in) (edging top/bottom), 2 rectangles g of 8 x 14.5cm (3¼ x 5¾in) (first strip in block), 2 rectangles h of 8 x 21cm (3¼ x 8¼in) (second strip in block), 2 rectangles i of 8 x 19cm (3¼ x 7½in) (loops)
- E: 2 rectangles g of 8 x 14.5cm (3¼ x 5¾in) (first strip in block), 2 rectangles h of 8 x 21cm (3¼ x 8¼in) (second strip in block), 2 rectangles i of 8 x 19cm (3¼ x 7½in) (loops)
- F: 2 rectangles g of 8 x 14.5cm (3¼ x 5¾in) (first strip in block), 2 rectangles h of 8 x 21cm (3¼ x 8¼in) (second strip in block), 2 rectangles i of 8 x 19cm (3¼ x 7½in) (loops)

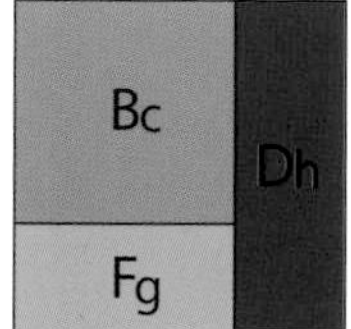
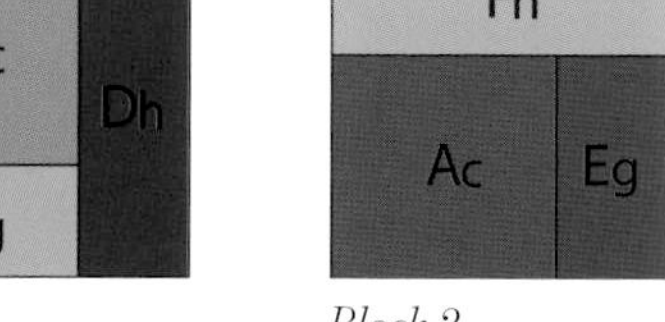

Block 1

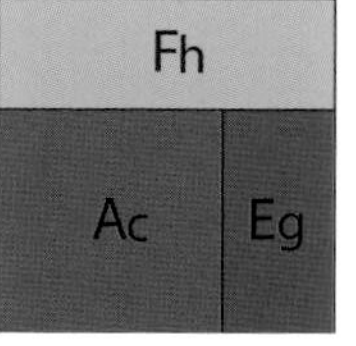

Block 2

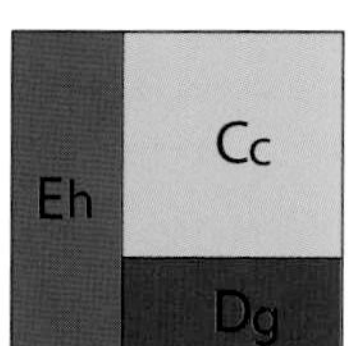
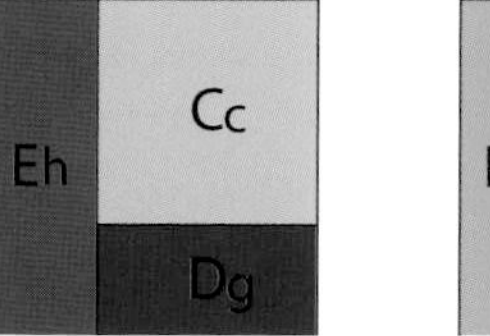

Block 3

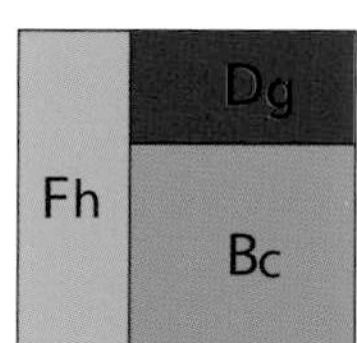

Block 4

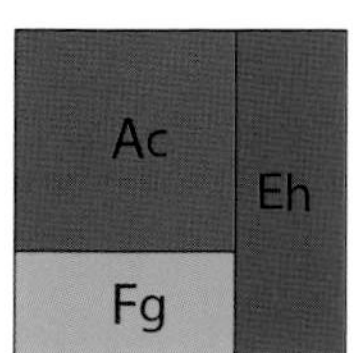

Block 5

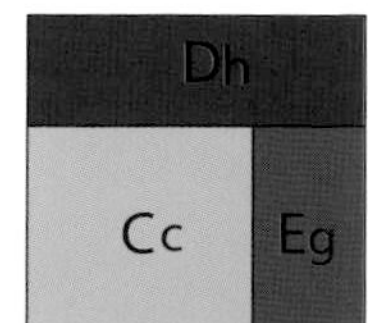

Block 6

1 For the pockets, fold all rectangles c together with wrong sides facing to 13.25 x 14.5cm (5¼ x 5¾in), then topstitch 1cm (½in) from the folded edge. Place the pockets on a pocket b in the same fabric and line up the bottom edge. Sew the first strip g to one side with the right sides facing (refer to the diagram). Press the seam allowance to the strip.

2 Sew the second strip h to one side with the right sides facing (refer to the diagram). Again, press the seam allowance to the strip. Continue like this to sew six blocks as per the diagram, then arrange in three rows of two blocks.

3 To join the pockets, sew two blocks together and press the seam allowances away from the pocket towards one of the strips of the adjoining block. Then sew the rows together and press all the seam allowances down. Sew strips e to the sides, then press the seam allowances to the outside. Sew strips f to the top and bottom, then again press the seam allowances to the outside.

4 Iron the fleece to the wrong side of the patchworked front, then iron the leather-like interfacing to the wrong side of rectangle d (the back of the wall tidy). Trim the overlaps. To make the loops, fold the six rectangles i in half lengthwise with the right sides facing, and sew up the long sides. Turn the strips right side out. Move the seam to the middle of the strip, then press and fold in half (the seam should be on the inside).

5 Place the front onto the back with the wrong sides facing. Stitch in the ditch along all the seams in a matching thread, starting with the seams in the blocks; then sew the rows and finally the edging. Trim the back to the size of the front.

6 Sew the loops evenly to the top back of the wall tidy, aligning the raw edges – the outer loops should sit about 3cm (1¼in) in from the side edges. For the binding, sew the short sides of the three strips a together with the right sides facing to make one long strip. Fold the strip in half lengthways with the wrong sides facing, then pin the raw edges around the back of the wall tidy, starting halfway up the left-hand side; leave about 10cm (4in) of extra binding free at the beginning.

7 When you reach the top-left corner, pinch then fold the border out by 90 degrees, as shown in the photo.

8 Then fold the strip down again, realigning the raw edges, and continue to pin along the top, over your sewn loops. Continue until the wall tidy has been edged all round, ensuring that the strip for the border is at least 10cm (4in) longer than required at the beginning and end. Sew the border with a 1cm (½in) seam allowance, finishing about 25cm (9¾in) from the beginning of the seam.

3

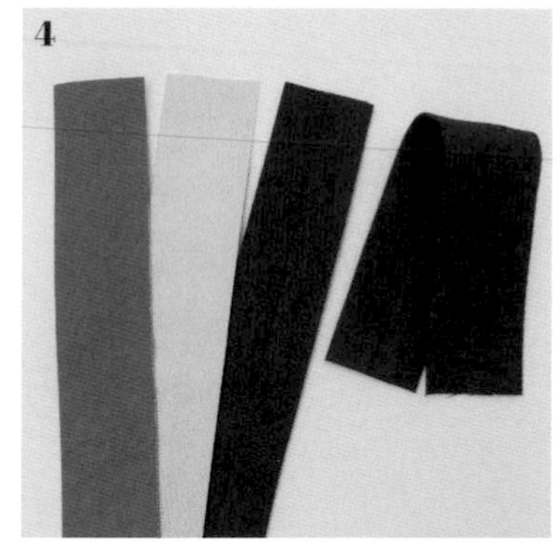
4

6

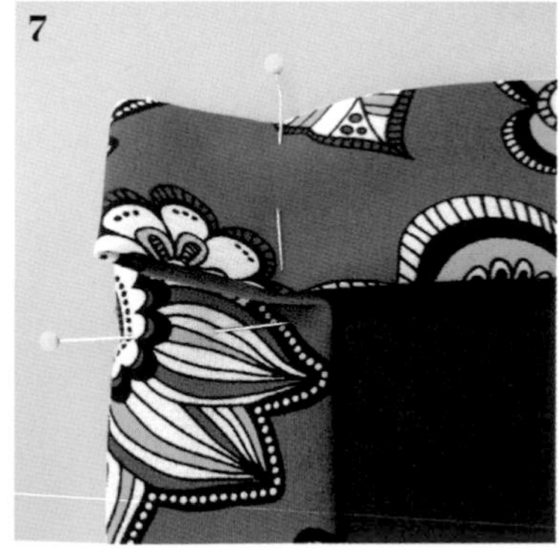
7

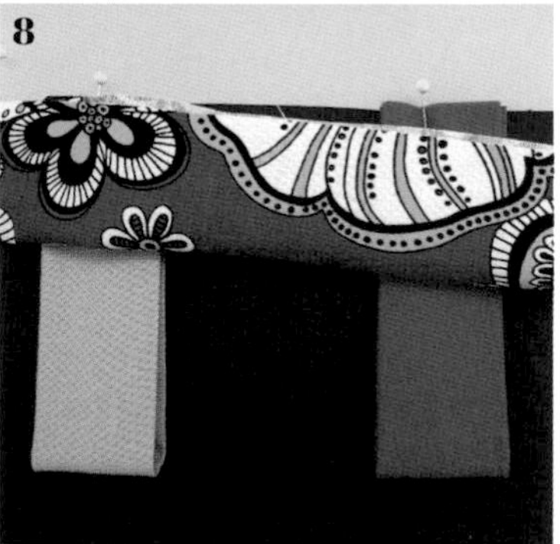
8

9 Bring the excess binding strips together. Insert a pin at the point where the fabrics meet.

10 Turn the border around the pin so they are at 90 degrees to each other, without removing or moving the pin. Use a pen to draw a line through the insertion point of the pin and sew the fabrics together along this line.

11 Check to make sure that the border is smooth. Trim the excess binding to the seam allowance width, as shown, then sew the remaining unsewn section of the border.

12 Fold the border over to the front all round and pin, laying the corners so that the folded edges are mitred. Edge stitch the folded edges from the front; fold the loops straight up along the top edge before stitching, so that they are sewn in place too.

10

11

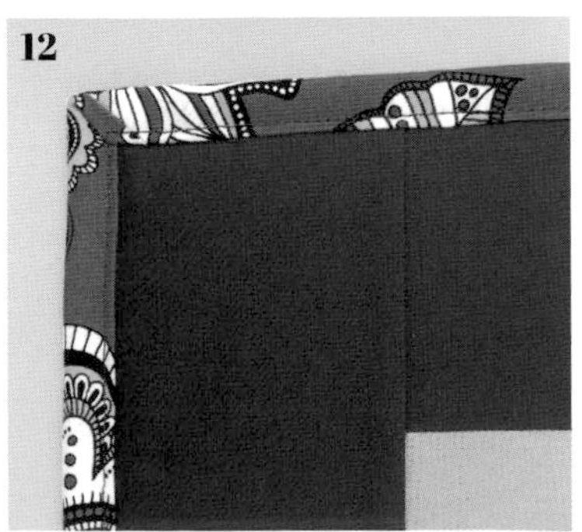

12

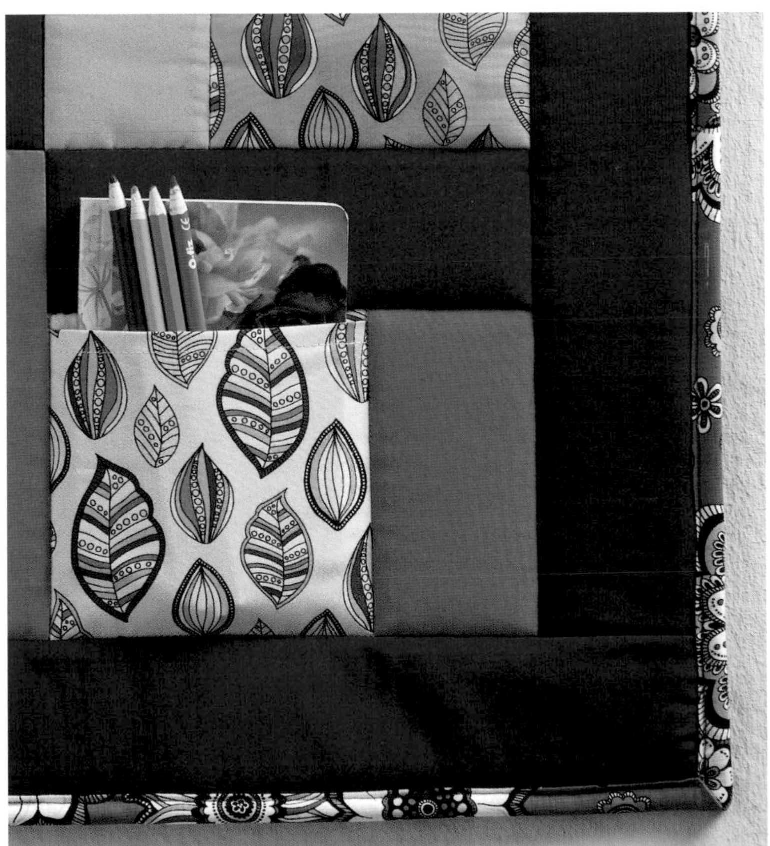

SIZE: 29 x 36CM (11½ x 14¼IN), PLUS HANDLES

LEVEL OF DIFFICULTY ♜

YOU WILL NEED

FABRIC:

- fine linen-mix patterned fabric for the outer, 81.5 x 91.5cm (32 x 36in)
- red cotton for the lining, 71 x 76.25cm (28 x 30in)

WADDING/BATTING AND INTERFACING:

- thin fusible wadding/batting, 71 x 76.25cm (28 x 30in)
- soft fusible interfacing, 15 x 81.5cm (6 x 32in)
- sturdy fusible interfacing, 20 x 30cm (8 x 12in)

ADDITIONAL ITEMS:

- 4 metal eyelets, 14mm (½in) in diameter
- templates, see page 189

CUTTING OUT

Add a 6mm (¼in) seam allowance to the bag and bag base patterns:

LINEN-MIX FABRIC:

- 2 bags
- 1 bag base
- 2 strips 7.5 x 81.5cm (3 x 32in) for the handles

RED COTTON LINING:

- 2 bags
- 1 bag base

THIN FUSIBLE WADDING/BATTING:

- 2 bags
- 1 bag base

SOFT FUSIBLE INTERFACING:

- 2 strips, 7.5 x 81.5cm (3 x 32in) for the handles

STURDY FUSIBLE INTERFACING:

- 1 bag base

Summer Bag

1 Back the three outer bag pieces with the corresponding wadding/batting pieces. Make pleats in the pieces as shown on the pattern (see the arrows) and tack/baste in place. Place the two bag pieces together with right sides facing and sew the side seams. Sew in the base, right sides facing.

2 Back the base lining piece with the sturdy fusible interfacing. Sew up the lining in the same way as the outer bag. When sewing the side seams together, leave a gap in one seam of about 15cm (6in) for turning out.

3 Iron a soft fusible interfacing strip to the wrong side of each fabric handle strip. At the ends of the handles, iron the seam allowances to the wrong side. Fold the handles lengthways, right sides together and sew the long sides together. Turn out and iron. Topstitch the edges if desired.

4 Put the outer bag inside the lining with right sides facing and seams and edges matching. Stitch around the top edge and trim the seam allowance back. Turn out the bag through the opening in the lining and carefully push out the top edge. Press and then topstitch all around, close to the edge. Sew up the opening in the lining with small hand stitches.

5 Attach the metal eyelets to the bag at the positions marked on the pattern, following the manufacturer's instructions. Thread the handles through the eyelets and tie a knot to secure each end.

SIZE: 40 x 80CM (15¾ x 31½IN)

LEVEL OF DIFFICULTY

YOU WILL NEED

FABRIC:

- A–P: 16 different cottons in rainbow colours for the pillow front, a, each 6.5 x 30cm (2½ x 11¾in) and 6 different strips b of 6.5 x 40cm (2½ x 15¾in) for the ties
- Q: cotton fabric in a black/charcoal pattern: 4 strips c of 6.5 x 110cm (2½ x 43¼in) for the front; 1 rectangle d of 31.5 x 81.5cm (12½ x 32in) for the back top; 1 rectangle e of 13 x 81.5cm (5 x 32in) for the back top facing; 2 rectangles f of 11.5 x 81.5cm (4½ x 32in) for the back bottom

WADDING/BATTING:

- thick iron-on volume fleece, 45 x 85cm (17¾ x 33½in)

ADDITIONAL ITEMS:

- 1 pillow pad, 40 x 80cm (15¾ x 31½in)

Rainbow Pillow

1 Cut all 16 fabrics A–P/a into 6.5cm (2½in) wide strips and arrange in a sequence of your choice.

2 Following the diagram and referring to the key, cut the strips A–P/a and Q/c into the lengths indicated (the dimensions include seam allowances). The dimensions for fabric Q also have 2cm (¾in) as a reserve, so that the finished front can be trimmed exactly to size later on and any unevenness corrected.

Continued overleaf...

2

KEY (FABRIC STRIPS Q/c):

a: 15cm (6in)
b: 12.5cm (5in)
c: 10cm (4in)
d: 16.5cm (6½in)
e: 11cm (4⅜in)
f: 14cm (5½in)
g: 13cm (5¼in)
h: 10.5cm (4¼in)
i: 8.5cm (3¾in)
j: 11.5cm (4½in)
k: 12cm (4¾in)
l: 15.5cm (6¼in)
m: 13.5cm (5⅜in)
n: 7.5cm (3in)

a	A: 21cm (8¼in)	b
b	B: 26cm (10¼in)	c
d	C: 17cm (6¾in)	a
c		e
f	E: 21.5cm (8½in)	g
h	F: 29.5cm (11½in)	i
b	G: 25cm (9¾in)	e
d	H: 17cm (6¾in)	a
j	I: 25cm (9¾in)	k
a	J: 17cm (6¾in)	d
b	K: 25.5cm (10in)	h
l	L: 19.5cm (7½in)	m
c	M: 28cm (11in)	h
g	N: 23cm (9in)	b
e	[illegible]	n
f	P: 19cm (7⅜in)	l

3 Sew the fabrics together in rows as per the diagram on page 74. Iron the seam allowances towards the central coloured strip. Sew the rows together to make the front of the pillow; iron the seam allowances as you like (but always in the same direction).

4 Iron the fusible fleece onto the back of your pillow front, trimming all round afterwards. Stitch in the ditch along all the strips in matching thread. Trim the finished front to exactly 41.5 x 81.5cm (16½ x 32in), making sure that the seams are parallel or at 90 degrees to the edges.

5 For the ties, fold strips b in half lengthwise with the wrong sides facing. Iron, then open out and fold the long sides into the middle. Iron the folds and fold the ties in half lengthways. Fold one short end to the inside by about 6mm (¼in) to neaten, then sew the folded edges together, working close to the edge.

6 For the top half of the back, pin the unfinished ends of three ties to one long right side of rectangle d; the outer ties are 20.5cm (8in) from the side edges. Pin the middle tie centrally in between. Pin rectangle e neatly on top with the right sides facing. Sew the edge together, sandwiching the ties in between.

7 Fold rectangle e to the wrong side of rectangle d. Shape the seam well, then iron and topstitch 6mm (¼in) from the seam. Fold the long unfinished fabric edge of rectangle e under twice and edge stitch it to rectangle d.

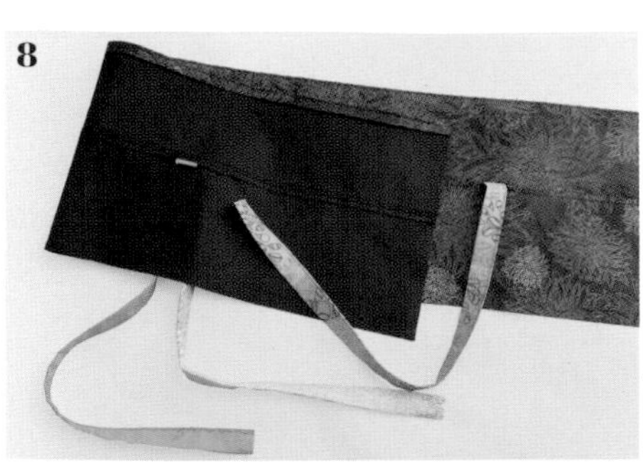

8

9

8 For the bottom part of the back, place the two rectangles f together with the right sides facing, and pin and then sew the remaining three ties between them, using the same spacing as for the other back piece. Open out the rectangles. Press the seam allowances over to the planned bottom edge. Edge stitch along the right side of the seam to finish the seam, making sure you don't accidentally sew over the ties.

9 Align the top and bottom back pieces, both with right sides facing up. Overlap them and tie the three sets of ties to make sure they are in the correct position. Pin together. Sew the two halves together along the side seams, taking a scant seam allowance.

10 Pin the pillow back to the pillow front with the right sides facing, making sure the ties are secured on the inside so they aren't accidentally sewn in. Sew the front and back together on all sides. Trim the corners at an angle. Turn the pillow cover right side out and shape the seams and corners well. Carefully press the seams on the back so they are flat.

11 Put the pad inside the cover and tie to secure.

10

11

SIZE: 27 x 23CM (10½ x 9IN)

LEVEL OF DIFFICULTY

YOU WILL NEED

Measure the height and width of your coffee pot, then add 5cm (2in) to each (mine measures 23cm (9in) tall including the lid, and 19cm (7½in) from spout to handle). The sizes below are for my coffee pot – adjust them as required for yours.

FABRIC:

- 2 pieces of outer fabric, 28 x 24cm (11 x 9½in)
- 2 pieces of lining fabric, 28 x 24cm (11 x 9½in)
- 2 strips of contrast fabric 1, 30.5 x 12.5cm (12 x 5in)
- 2 strips of contrast fabric 2, 12.5 x 25cm (5 x 10in)
- 2 strips of contrast fabric 3, 7.5 x 12.5cm (3 x 5in)

WADDING/BATTING:

- 2 pieces of thermal fleece, 28 x 24cm (11 x 9½in)

ADDITIONAL ITEMS:

- 2.5cm (1in) wide bias binding, 61cm (24in)
- 6mm (¼in) wide piping cord, 71cm (28in)
- 4cm (1½in) wide bias binding, 71cm (28in)
- 2 buttons to decorate, one larger than the other (optional)
- 30.5cm (12in) plate to use as a template
- hand sewing needle and thick thread
- water-soluble fabric marker pen

Contrast Coffee Cosy

1 For each side of the cosy, place the outer fabric on top of the wadding/batting and sew parallel straight lines across to quilt – as many as you like, and with no particular width apart. On one outer piece, lay contrast fabric 1 right side down at a diagonal angle, about 12.5cm (5in) from the bottom left corner as shown, and sew along the lower long edge.

2 Flip the contrast fabric over, and press. Sew straight lines through all the layers, again, no particular width apart.

Continued overleaf...

3

6

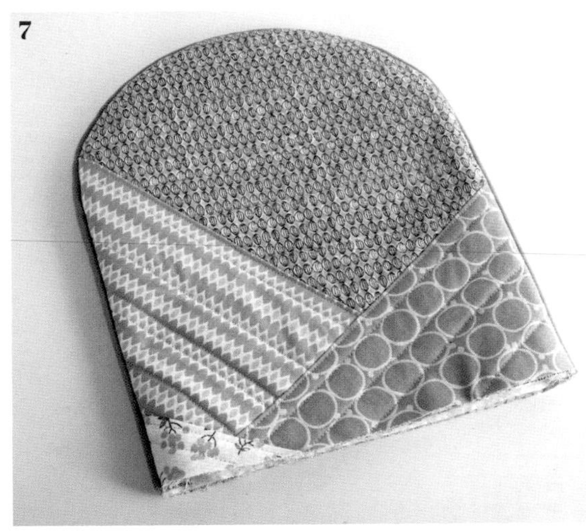

7

3 Place contrast fabric 2 right side down in the opposite direction (as shown), and sew as before.

4 Flip over contrast fabric 2, and quilt as before. Add contrast fabric 3 to the bottom-left corner in the same way, then quilt.

5 Repeat steps 1–4 for the other outer piece. Trim away the excess fabric at the edges. Using your plate as a template, draw then cut the rounded shape of the top of the cosy. Make sure both outer pieces are the same shape. Trim the lining to match.

6 Open out and then wrap the 4cm (1½in) wide bias binding around the piping cord. Sew the fabric in place along the length (see page 27). Snip into the seam allowance of the bias binding to allow it to curve, then pin and sew it raw edge to raw edge to the sides and curved top of one outer piece. Trim any excess piping.

7 Place the second outer piece on top, right sides together, and sew around the sides and curved top, close to the piping. Turn the cosy right side out and press. Add the buttons at this point, if desired.

8 Sew the two lining pieces right sides together, around the sides and curved top. Leave the lining inside out.

9 Push the lining inside the cosy, wrong sides together, and sew together all around the bottom of the cosy, very close to the edge. This helps to keep the fabrics in place while you add the bias binding at the bottom. Sew the 2.5cm (1in) bias binding around the bottom of the cosy (see page 21).

SIZE: 43 x 35CM (17 x 13¾IN), WITHOUT HANDLES

LEVEL OF DIFFICULTY

YOU WILL NEED

FABRIC:

- A: cream cotton, 45 x 110cm (17¾ x 43¼in)
- B: light green patterned cotton, 50 x 110cm (19¾ x 43¼in)
- C–E: 3 different cottons in light blue/turquoise/green, each 10 x 40cm (4 x 15¾in)
- F: light blue cotton, 20 x 110cm (8 x 43¼in)

WADDING/BATTING:

- G: thin iron-on volume fleece, 45 x 90cm (17¾ x 35½in)

CUTTING OUT

Dimensions include an 8mm (3/8in) seam allowance:

- A: 2 rectangles a of 8.5 x 36.5cm (3½ x 14½in) for the bag bottom outer; 2 rectangles b of 22.5 x 36.5cm (9 x 14½in) for the bag top outer; 2 strips c of 5.5 x 70cm (2¼ x 27½in) for the handles
- B: 2 rectangles d of 45 x 36.5cm (17¾ x 14½in) for the lining; 4 squares e of 8.5 x 8.5cm (3½ x 3½in) for the patchwork
- C–E: 4 squares e of 8.5 x 8.5cm (3½ x 3½in) for the patchwork
- F: 2 strips c of 5.5 x 70cm (2¼ x 27½in) for the handles; 4 squares e of 8.5 x 8.5cm (3½ x 3½in) for the patchwork
- G: 2 strips c of 5.5 x 70cm (2¼ x 27½in) for the handles; 2 pieces f of 44 x 37cm (17¼ x 14½in) for the bag outer

Shopping Bag

1 For the two patchwork sections, lay the 20 squares e (fabrics B–F) into four separate rows of five squares and sew the squares together with the right sides facing. Press the seam allowances for the top and bottom rows of each patchwork section in opposite directions.

2 Sew the rows together in pairs with right sides facing, pinning the vertical seams together first so they are lined up perfectly. Open out and press.

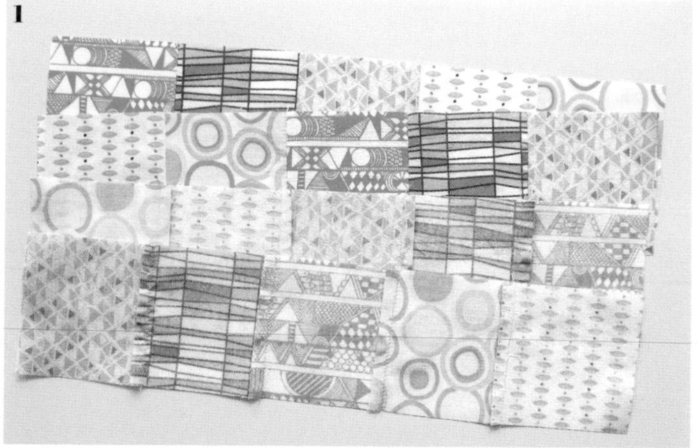

1

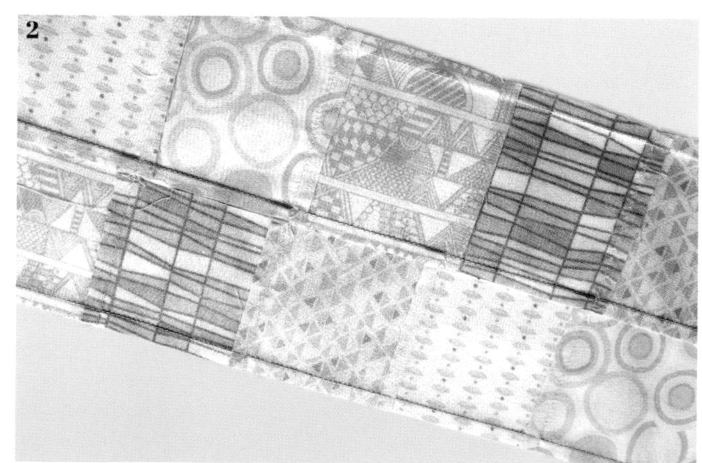

2

Continued overleaf...

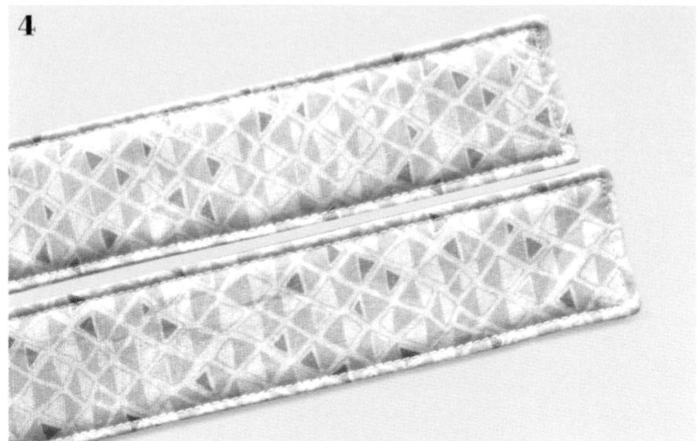

3 For each patchwork section, sew one rectangle A/a to the bottom edge and one rectangle A/b to the top edge. Iron the seam allowances of the patchwork towards the newly sewn-on pieces. Iron the fleece pieces G/f to the back of the bag outer pieces and trim the fleece to size. Stitch in the ditch around the squares, sewing the horizontal seams first and then the vertical ones. Secure the beginnings and ends of the vertical seams.

4 For the two handles, iron the strips F/c onto fleece G/c and trim the fleece to size. Place strips F/c and A/c right sides together and sew all around, leaving a turning gap of about 15cm (6in) in one long side. Trim the corner seam allowances at an angle and turn the handles right side out. Work the corners and side seams out well and then press. Edge stitch all around.

5 Pin the two ends of one handle to the right side of one outer bag piece; the ends should sit 14cm (5½in) down from the top edge and 9cm (3½in) in from the side edges. Sew the ends in place along the handle edge stitching, sewing across the handle 3cm (1¼in) from the top. Repeat for the other handle on the other outer bag piece.

6 Place the outer bag pieces together with the right sides facing, making sure the horizontal seams of the patchwork are lined up, then pin. Sew along the side and bottom edges.

7

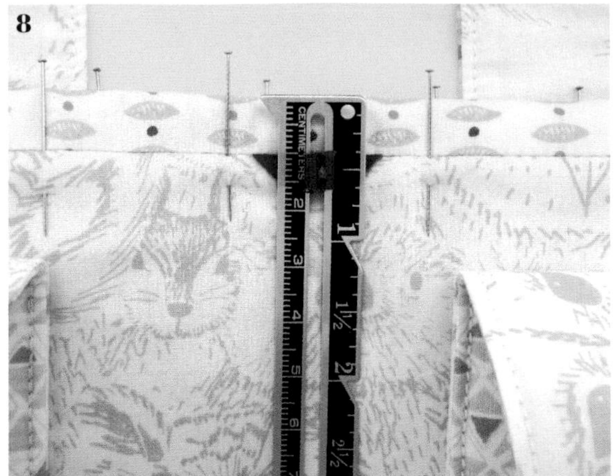
8

7 For the lining, place the two rectangles B/d together with right sides facing. Sew along the long sides and the bottom edge, leaving a turning opening of about 15cm (6in) in one side edge. For the base corners of the outer piece and lining, align the side seams over the base seam, then sew the corner diagonally, 3cm (1¼in) from the side/bottom seam. Trim the base corners back to the seam allowance (see page 16).

8 Turn the lining right side out and put inside the outer piece so the right sides are together. Line up the top edges and side seams and pin. Sew all around the top edges of the outer piece and lining. Turn the bag right side out through the opening in the lining and shape the corners well. Fold the seam allowances of the turning opening to the inside and edge stitch along the opening with your machine. Arrange the lining so that about 1cm (½in) protrudes up above the top seam, creating a faux binding; pin in place.

9 Secure the top edge by stitching in the ditch of the existing seam all round. Increase the stitch length slightly to 3mm (⅛in). Your bag is complete!

9

TEA TOWEL: 44 x 58CM (17¼ x 23IN)

OVEN MITT: 20 x 28CM (8 x 11IN)

LEVEL OF DIFFICULTY ♜♜

YOU WILL NEED

FABRIC FOR THE TEA TOWEL:

- denim for the outer, 46 x 60cm (18¼ x 24in)
- red cotton for the apple, 10 x 10cm (4 x 4in)
- scraps of green cotton for the leaves
- cream cotton for the apple core, 10 x 10cm (4 x 4in)
- grey cotton for the trim, 46 x 15cm (18¼ x 6in)

INTERFACING FOR THE TEA TOWEL:

- woven, medium-weight, fusible, 46 x 15cm (18¼ x 6in)

FABRIC FOR THE OVEN MITT:

- denim for the outer, 60 x 35cm (24 x 13¾in)
- red cotton for the lining, 60 x 35cm (24 x 13¾in)
- scrap of green cotton for the leaves
- scrap of red cotton for the apple
- scrap of cream cotton for the core
- grey cotton for the trim, 6.5 x 20cm (2½ x 8in)

WADDING/BATTING FOR THE OVEN MITT:

- dense polyester, insulated fleece, 60 x 35cm (24 x 13¾in)

ADDITIONAL ITEMS:

- black and white bakers' string/twine or other cord for a hanging loop
- black thread for FME
- coordinating thread for the quilting
- fabric glue stick
- water-soluble marker pen
- embroidery hoop for FME (optional)
- templates, see page 190

Apple Kitchen Set

TEA TOWEL

1 Fuse the interfacing to the back of the grey trim.

2 Using the templates on page 190, cut out the apple, core and leaves from their corresponding fabrics and glue them onto the centre of the trim. Draw on the outlines of the seeds and stalk with the water-soluble marker.

3 Set up your machine for free-motion embroidery then embroider on the apple details with black thread. Start with the edges to secure the apple pieces and end with the seeds.

4 Trim away the threads and then mist the trim to remove the marker lines. Fold the two long ends under by 6mm (¼in) and press. Lay the trim onto the towel, 12cm (4¾in) up from one end, and pin.

5 Swap to the coordinating thread and attach the trim by topstitching close to the edge.

6 Double hem the towel: fold the edges to the wrong side by 1cm (½in) and press. Then turn the edges under again by 1cm (½in). Stitch in place, then press.

Continued overleaf...

OVEN MITT

1 Cut two pieces of denim fabric, each 30 x 35cm (12 x 13¾in). Using the template and water-soluble marker, draw the mitt shape onto them (as mirror images of each other). Do not cut them out yet.

2 Cut two pieces of insulated wadding/batting to the same size as the denim, then lay your denim fabric pieces on top.

3 For the back mitt piece, use a coordinating thread and quilt a random wavy pattern. Take the quilting lines slightly over the mitt outline. Cut the back piece out.

4 Take your piece of trim measuring 6.5 x 20cm (2½ x 8in) and turn the long edges under by 6mm (¼in); press. Lay this trim onto the mitt, as shown on the template, and topstitch it on with coordinating thread. Using the templates, cut out the apple, core and leaves from their corresponding fabrics and glue them onto the centre of the trim. Draw on the outlines of the seeds and stalk with the water-soluble marker. Stitch the outlines with free-motion embroidery. Cut out the mitt.

5 Using the mitt template once again, cut out two pieces of red lining fabric, as mirror images of each other.

6 Cut a piece of bakers' string/twine, about 25cm (10in) in length, and fold it in half. Attach this as marked on the template (the cross) to form a hanging loop.

7 Place the two mitt outers right sides together and sew around the perimeter, leaving the bottom straight edge unsewn. Sew the lining in the same way, leaving a turning gap in the longest, straightest section of the mitt.

8 With the outer the right way out and the lining inside out, pull the lining on over the outer. Sew around the straight bottom edge and then turn out through the gap. Close up the gap with hand stitches.

9 Stuff the lining down into the mitt and topstitch the straight bottom edge with coordinating threads.

Tip

Be very sure to draw the mitt pieces (both lining and outer) with one as a mirror image of the other! Either draw once, flip the template and draw again, or fold the fabric right sides together and then draw and cut the shapes out once.

SIZE: 40 x 20CM (16 x 8IN)

LEVEL OF DIFFICULTY

YOU WILL NEED

FABRIC:

- floral outer fabric, 80 x 32cm (31½ x 12½in)
- checked lining fabric, 80 x 45cm (31½ x 18in)

WADDING/BATTING AND INTERFACING:

- fusible wadding/batting, 80 x 40cm (31½ x 15¾in)
- firm fusible pelmet interfacing, 80 x 40cm (31½ x 15¾in)

ADDITIONAL ITEMS:

- circular metal clip handle
- template, see page 191

CUTTING OUT

Add a 1cm (⅜in) seam allowance all round the template on page 191. The other measurements given below include the necessary seam allowances:

FLORAL FABRIC:

- 2 bag pieces, for the outer bag
- 1 strip 80 x 15cm (31½ x 6in), for the base/sides
- 2 strips 32 x 8cm (12½ x 3¼in), for the handle channels

CHECKED FABRIC:

- 2 bag pieces for the lining
- 1 strip 80 x 15cm (31½ x 6in), for the base/side lining
- 1 rectangle 20 x 30cm (8 x 12in), for the inside pocket

FUSIBLE WADDING/BATTING:

- 2 bag pieces
- 1 strip 80 x 15cm (31½ x 6in), for the base/sides

FIRM FUSIBLE PELMET INTERFACING:

- 2 bag pieces
- 1 strip 80 x 15cm (31½ x 6in), for the base/sides

Fun and Flirty Bag

1 Fuse the wadding/batting to the back of the corresponding outer front, back and base/side pieces. Fuse the interfacing to the back of the corresponding lining front, back and base/side pieces.

2 Fold the pocket rectangle in half widthways with right sides facing, so it is 20 x 15cm (8 x 6in). Sew together the open edges, leaving a gap in the seam on one side for turning out. Trim the seam allowances at the corners, then turn out the pocket, pushing out the corners carefully. Close up the opening with small hand stitches. Topstitch the pocket on one long edge, using the presser foot as a guide – this will be the top edge. Pin the pocket centrally to the right side of one bag lining piece, then stitch it in place around the sides and bottom edge.

3 Stitch one long edge of the wadded base/side piece to one wadded bag outer piece, right sides facing and aligning the raw edges. Attach the other outer piece in the same way.

4 Assemble the lining pieces in the same way, but leave a gap in one seam for turning out. Make sure the stitches are secured on either side of the gap. Turn the lining right side out.

5 Hem each short end of the two handle channel strips by turning the edges of the fabric to the wrong side twice by 1cm (⅜in) then sewing in place. Fold each strip in half lengthways, wrong sides together, and topstitch 2.5cm (1in) from the fold and parallel to it. With right sides facing, centre each channel on the wadded front and back pieces, with the long raw edges flush to the bag's top raw edges; tack/baste in place. Turn the bag inside out.

6 Place the lining into the bag, right sides together, matching the raw edges. Sew along the top edge, catching the channels for the handles at the same time. Turn the bag out through the opening in the lining and close up the opening with small hand stitches. Push the lining into the bag. Topstitch the edge of the bag using the width of the presser foot as a guide.

7 Guide the long pins of the bag handles through the channels, place the screws on the ends and tighten up.

ESIGERE
LA MARCA
PASTIGLIE
AROMATICHE
HIMBEERPASTILLEN
DISSETANTI
LEONE
DITTA L. LEONE

SIZE: 22 x 16CM (8¾ x 6¼IN)

LEVEL OF DIFFICULTY

YOU WILL NEED

FABRIC:

- pink checked cotton for the main front panel, 14 x 16cm (5½ x 6¼in)
- pink cotton for the back, 22 x 16cm (8¾ x 6¼in)
- pink floral cotton for the front side panel, 9.5 x 16cm (3¾ x 6¼in)
- pink striped cotton for the binding, 6.5 x 92cm (2½ x 36¼in)
- scraps of pink patterned cotton

WADDING/BATTING:

- 22 x 16cm (8¾ x 6¼in)

ADDITIONAL ITEMS:

- fusible webbing, 10cm (4in)
- white crochet trim, 20cm (8in)
- pink rickrack braid, 20cm (8in)
- green ribbon, 25cm (10in)
- green variegated thread
- templates, see page 192

Nostalgic Charm Mug Rug

1 Sew the main front and front side panel pieces together along the 16cm (6¼in) edges with right sides facing, then press the seam open. Draw around the flower and flower centre templates onto the fusible webbing and cut out, leaving a generous margin all round. Iron the flower and its centre onto the back of the patterned fabric scraps. Cut out the pieces, arrange them on the main front panel and iron to fuse in place. Pin the front, wadding/batting and back pieces together with right sides out.

2 Embroider the edges of the flower and its centre using a decorative machine stitch and green variegated thread, or work in blanket stitch by hand. Emphasize the seam between the two front pieces with the same stitch. Sew the crochet trim to the seam. Sew the rickrack braid 2.5cm (1in) from the seam, over the front side panel, using a small machine zigzag. Attach the ribbon 2cm (¾in) from the top edge using a large zigzag or any embroidery stitch on your sewing machine.

3 Edge the mug rug with the pink striped binding strips (see page 21).

Tip

Most modern sewing machines have a wide range of embroidery stitches, and they can be used in many different ways – not just to neaten an appliqué, but also as an alternative quilting stitch. Use multicoloured, variegated or contrasting thread for a special effect on plain fabrics to emphasize a seam, or provide support for a sewn-on trim.

Opposite:
Mug rug with appliquéd flower by Renate Bieber.

SIZE: 29 x 27CM (11½ x 10½IN)

LEVEL OF DIFFICULTY

YOU WILL NEED

For a teapot measuring 25.5cm (10in) across:

FABRIC:

- 2 pieces of outer fabric, 30.5 x 28cm (12 x 11in)
- 2 pieces of lining fabric, 30.5 x 28cm (12 x 11in)
- 25.5cm (10in) square of fabric for the semicircle appliqué
- patterned fabric scraps backed with fusible adhesive, each about 10cm (4in) square

WADDING/BATTING:

- 2 pieces of thermal wadding/batting, 30.5 x 28cm (12 x 11in)

ADDITIONAL ITEMS:

- water-soluble fabric marker pen
- 2.5cm (1in) wide bias binding, 66cm (26in)
- 24cm (9½in) circle template (I used a large plate)
- 15cm (6in) circle template (I used a small side plate)
- templates, see page 192

Flower Tea Cosy

1 Using the smaller circle template, round off the two top corners of the outer fabrics, lining fabrics and wadding/batting into curves.

2 Draw an arc on the front outer fabric with the water-soluble pen, using the large circle template. Use the templates on page 192 to cut out appliqué shapes from your fusible fabric scraps; arrange them around the arc, then iron in place. Draw stalks from the appliqué shapes, connecting them to the arc. In addition, draw a bird tail. Place the outer fabric on top of the wadding/batting, and free-motion embroider the shapes and stalks in a contrasting thread.

3 Fold the square fabric in half. Draw a semicircle with the large circle template, with the fold of the fabric just above the top of the arc. Cut 6mm (¼in) beyond your drawn line to create two semi-circles. Sew the shapes right sides together along the curve, leaving the straight edge open. Snip into the curve, turn right side out and press.

4 Place the semi-circle over the front fabric, and sew a few concentric arcs to quilt in place.

5 Pin the remaining wadding/batting to the wrong side of the plain outer fabric piece. Place the two outer pieces right sides together and sew around the curve, leaving the straight edge open. Snip into the curve, turn right side out and press.

6 Sew the two lining pieces together around the curved side. Push the lining, inside out, inside the tea cosy and tack/baste the raw edges together.

7 Apply the bias binding around the raw edge (see page 21).

2

7

Sewing Machine Cover

SIZE: 44 x 30 x 19CM (17½ x 12 x 7½IN)

LEVEL OF DIFFICULTY

YOU WILL NEED

Measure the height, depth and width (at its widest part) of your sewing machine and add 4cm (1½in) to each measurement. Mine is 43cm (17in) wide, 29cm (11½in) high and 18cm (7in) deep. If your machine is a different size, adjust the measurements below accordingly.

FABRIC:

- 2 pieces of outer fabric, 47 x 33cm (18½ x 13in) for the front and back
- 2 pieces of lining fabric, 46.5 x 33cm (18¼ x 13in)
- 2 pieces of outer fabric, 21.5 x 33cm (8½ x 13in) for the sides
- 2 pieces of lining fabric, 21 x 33cm (8¼ x 13in)
- 1 piece of outer fabric, 47 x 21.5cm (18½ x 8½in) for the top
- 1 piece of lining fabric, 46.5 x 21cm (18¼ x 8¼in)
- 1 piece of floral fabric, 25.5 x 10cm (10 x 4in) for the handle
- 4 pieces of floral fabric, 47 x 15cm (18½ x 6in) for the side pockets
- 4 pieces of floral fabric, 21.5 x 15cm (8½ x 6in) for the side pockets

FOAM STABILIZER:

- 2 pieces of foam stabilizer, 47 x 33cm (18½ x 13in), for the front and back
- 2 pieces of foam stabilizer, 21.5 x 33cm (8½ x 13in), for the sides
- 1 piece of foam stabilizer, 47 x 21.5cm (18½ x 8½in), for the top
- 1 piece of foam stabilizer, 20.5 x 5cm (8 x 2in) for the handle

ADDITIONAL ITEMS:

- 2 buttons
- 2.5cm (1in) wide bias binding, 3m (3¼yd)
- ruler
- water-soluble fabric marker pen

1 Take each outer fabric piece and, starting in the centre, draw diagonal 60-degree quilting guidelines, 4cm (1½in) apart. Draw lines in the opposite direction to make a grid of diamonds. Place each piece of outer fabric over its corresponding foam piece and topstitch along the lines.

2 With the wrong sides facing, pin the pocket pieces together in pairs, then sew the bias binding to the top edge (see page 21). Tack/baste the pockets to the bottoms of the quilted outer pieces. Topstitch dividing lines on some or all of the pockets to make compartments any size you like.

3 Sew the front, back and side outer pieces right sides together along the 33cm (13in) edges to make a tube. Turn right side out. Topstitch closely along each side of the seams, to help them stay in shape.

1

2

4 Wrap the handle fabric around the foam, tucking in all the raw edges, then topstitch all the way round. Position this centrally on the top of the cover, lifting it slightly to make an arc shape; pin then sew at each end, then attach a button over your stitches.

5 With the cover inside out again, pin then sew in the top. Turn right side out.

6 Make up the lining in the same way, then drop inside the cover, wrong sides together, and tack/baste around the bottom edge. Add bias binding to finish (see page 21).

SIZE: 4.5 x 6CM (1¾ x 2¼IN)

LEVEL OF DIFFICULTY

YOU WILL NEED

FABRIC FOR ONE KEY RING:

- A: strawberry patterned fabric for the front/back, 20 x 10cm (8 x 4in)
- B: polka dot patterned fabric for the lining, 9 x 10cm (3½ x 4in)

WADDING/BATTING FOR ONE KEY RING:

- C: medium iron-on volume fleece, 13 x 7cm (5 x 3½in)

ADDITIONAL ITEMS FOR ONE KEY RING:

- red hook-and-loop fastening, 1.5cm (½in)
- cotton webbing in pink and red, 4.5cm (1¾in)
- 1 key ring, 3cm (1¼in) diameter
- sewing thread in pink and red

CUTTING OUT

Dimensions include a 6mm (¼in) seam allowance:

- A: 1 rectangle a of 9 x 7cm (3½ x 2¾in) for the pocket front; 1 rectangle b of 8.5 x 7cm (3¼ x 2¾in)
- B: 1 rectangle b of 8.5 x 7cm (3¼ x 2¾in)
- C: 1 rectangle b of 8.5 x 7cm (3¼ x 2¾in); 1 rectangle c of 4.5 x 7cm (1¾ x 2¾in)

Fabric Purse Keyrings

1 Fold fabric A/a in half wrong sides together (to measure 4.5 x 7cm/1¾ x 2¾in), press, then insert fleece C/c between the fold. Fold the cotton webbing into a loop and pin right sides facing just under the long top edge on the right-hand side. Edgestitch down the right-hand side, across the bottom and up to the top folded edge.

2 Place the hook side of the hook-and-loop fastener on the centre of the A/a fabric, 6mm (¼in) from the top edge, and sew in place to complete the pocket front.

3 Place fabric B/b on fleece C/b, and the pocket front A/a on top, aligning the bottom edges. Place fabric A/b on top, right sides facing.

4 Sew around the sides and top edge. Trim the corner seam allowances at an angle and turn the key holder right side out, so that the entire lining piece B/b is visible, with A/a facing A/b.

5 Carefully shape the corners and smooth the fabric.

6 Sew up the turning opening approximately 6mm (¼in) above the bottom edge. Neaten with zigzag stitch and turn the 'pocket' right side out. Press, and place the fleecy part of the hook-and-loop fastening on the middle of the flap on the inside. Sew 1cm (½in) from the top edge. Pull the key ring through the cotton webbing.

M49
and
20 Mittwoch
21 Donnerstag
22 Freitag
23 Samstag
24 Sonntag

SIZE: 24 x 13 x 16CM (9½ x 5 x 6½IN)

LEVEL OF DIFFICULTY

YOU WILL NEED

Measure the height, width and depth of your toaster and add 4cm (1½in) to each measurement. My toaster is 23cm (9in) long, 11.5cm (4½in) wide and 15cm (6in) high, so the cover is based on this size.

FABRIC:

- 4 pieces of plain fabric (mine has a slight spot detail) for the outer and lining front and back, 19 x 26.5cm (7½ x 10½in)
- 2 pieces of plain fabric for the outer and lining top/sides, 15 x 56cm (6 x 22in)
- 2 pieces of striped fabric, 26.5 x 9cm (10½ x 3½in)
- 2 pieces of striped fabric, 15 x 9cm (6 x 3½in)
- 1 piece of coloured fabric for the door, 7.5 x 13cm (3 x 5in)
- 4 pieces of cream fabric for the windows, 10 x 7.5cm (4 x 3in)
- 1 piece of cream fabric for the door window, 5cm (2in) square
- 1 piece of spotty fabric for the plant pot, 2.5 x 5cm (1 x 2in)
- 8 pieces of floral fabric for the curtains, 5 x 7.5cm (2 x 3in)
- 2 pieces of floral fabric for the door curtains, 5cm (2in) square

WADDING/BATTING:

- 2 pieces of wadding/batting, 19 x 26.5cm (7½ x 10½in)
- 1 piece of wadding/batting, 15 x 56cm (6 x 22in)

ADDITIONAL ITEMS:

- 8 small buttons to tie back the curtains
- 1 button for the door handle
- 3 flower-shaped buttons
- repositionable spray fabric adhesive
- 5cm (2in) circle template
- water-soluble fabric marker pen

Caravan Toaster Cover

1 Fold over the top long edges of the four striped pieces of fabric to the wrong side by 1cm (½in) and press.

2 Place the two wider pieces of striped fabric over the bottoms of the two plain 19 x 26.5cm (7½ x 10½in) rectangles and topstitch the pressed edges. Lay these pieces on top of the corresponding wadding/batting pieces. One will be the front and one will be the back of your caravan.

3 Draw horizontal lines with your water-soluble pen at 1cm (½in) intervals from the top of the striped fabric to the top of the plain fabric, then sew to quilt the layers together. Using your circle template, round off the two top corners.

4 Take the plain outer top/sides piece and place the corresponding piece of striped fabric over one end. Topstitch the pressed edge. Add the same number of quilting lines as in step 3.

Continued overleaf...

3

5 Spray the back of one window piece with fabric adhesive and position it overlapping the striped fabric slightly, as shown. Fold two pieces of curtain fabric in half, right sides facing, and press. Place these, raw edges together, at the sides of the window. Fold back the edges as shown and satin stitch all the way round the window. Sew a button onto each curtain. Don't put the window on the opposite end just yet.

6 Repeat step 5 to add a window to the back of the caravan, slightly to one side.

14

7 Repeat again with the window on the front of the caravan, placing it to one side so there is room for the pot and door, as shown.

8 Add the door, and satin stitch all the way round. Using your 5cm (2in) circle template, round off the top of the door window. Fold the two pieces of door curtain fabric in half and press, then place them over the door window and cut to the same shape. Satin stitch to secure. Add a button for the door handle.

9 Trim the bottom corners of the plant-pot fabric to make a cone shape, and satin stitch to the side of the door. Draw stalks with your erasable pen, then stitch over these with a bold triple stitch on your machine, before adding your flower buttons.

10 Pin the front of the caravan to the window side of the top/sides piece, lining up the striped sections and with right sides facing. Keep pinning all the way around the caravan front, and trim any extra fabric when you come to the other end. This ensures your top/sides panel is cut to the right length.

11 Unpin, then sew the striped panel, quilting lines, window and curtains onto the other end of the top/sides piece.

12 Sew the front and back of the caravan, right sides together, to the top/sides piece.

13 Sew the remaining lining pieces together in the same way, leaving a gap in one side of about 10cm (4in) for turning.

14 Drop the outer fabric inside the lining, right sides together, and sew the bottom raw edges together. Turn right side out through the gap in the lining and then stitch the gap closed by hand or machine.

15 Push the lining inside the outer layer, press, then topstitch around the hem.

SIZE: 12CM (4¾IN) ACROSS

LEVEL OF DIFFICULTY

YOU WILL NEED

FABRIC:

- printed cotton for the outer and lining, 25.5 x 25.5cm (10 x 10in)

WADDING/BATTING:

- thin, iron-on fleece, 13 x 38cm (5 x 15in)

ADDITIONAL ITEMS:

- 1 zip, 10cm (4in)
- bias binding in a matching colour, 40cm (16in)
- template, see page 193

CUTTING OUT

- 4 circles of printed cotton fabric using the template – one is for a lining so it can be a different fabric
- 3 pieces of fleece wadding/ batting using the template

Coin Purse

1 Iron fleece wadding/batting onto the wrong sides of three circles of printed cotton fabric. Fold two pieces in half with the wrong sides facing and press.

2 Push the zip tape under the fold of one of the folded pieces and edge stitch using the zipper foot on your sewing machine. Sew the other folded piece onto the other side of the zip in the same way.

3 Position the unfolded, fleece-backed piece of printed cotton fabric right side down, then place the fourth piece on top of it, wrong sides facing. Then place the front fabric piece (with the zip) on top; the right side should be facing up. Stitch around the edges of the whole piece with a zigzag stitch.

4 Sew bias binding all round the edge of the purse, using topstitch to finish (see page 21).

10 EURO CENT
20 EURO CENT
NEDERLANDEN BEATRIX

SIZE: 16.5 x 10CM (6½ x 4IN)

LEVEL OF DIFFICULTY

Button Heart

YOU WILL NEED

FABRIC:

- linen, 30 x 22cm (12 x 8½in)

ADDITIONAL ITEMS:

- template, see page 194
- twine, about 35cm (14in) long
- small mother-of-pearl buttons
- small amount of stuffing

1 Fold the linen in half, right sides together. Pin on the template, then cut out to create two pieces.

2 Knot the ends of the twine together to make a loop. Pin the two heart shapes together, right sides facing, and trap the twine loop between the layers with the loop end sticking out of the top. Sew the hearts together with a 1cm (½in) seam allowance, leaving a 5cm (2in) gap for turning on one straight side. Remember to back-tack at the beginning and end of the stitch line. Clip the curves and the point of the heart.

3 Turn right side out and roll the seams gently to improve the shape. Stuff with small pieces of stuffing, then hand-sew the opening closed.

4 Sew the first button about 2cm (¾in) below the twine loop. Sew a second button at the point of the heart. Sew a third and fourth button at the midway point on each side of the heart to create a framework for the button outline.

5 Complete the button outline, keeping approximately 2cm (¾in) from the seam line of the heart.

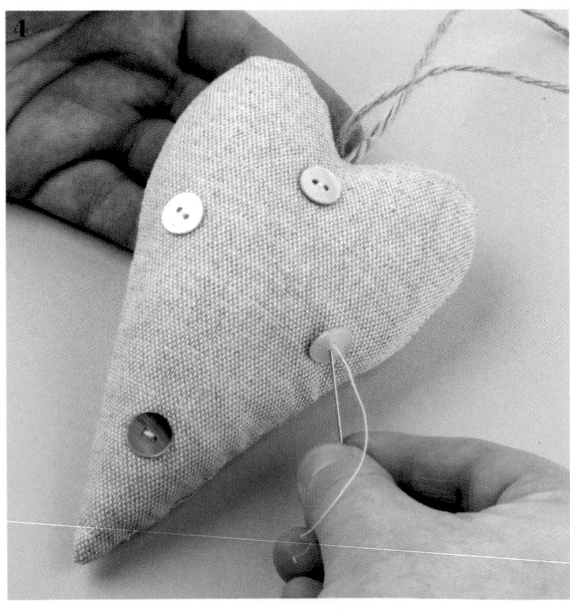
4

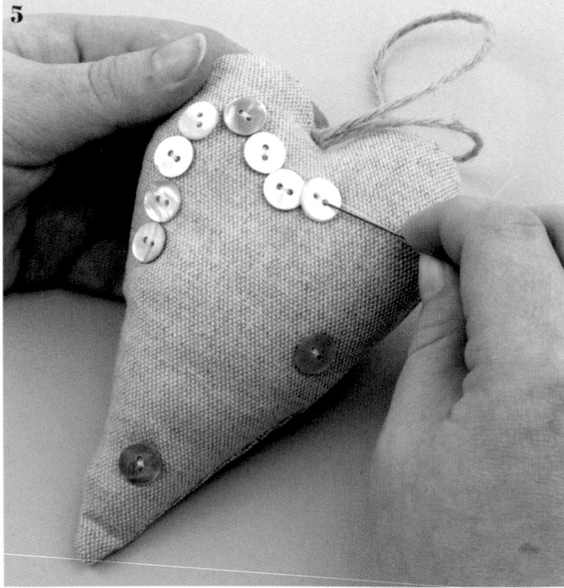
5

SIZE: ABOUT 30 x 42CM (12 x 16½IN), PLUS HOOK

LEVEL OF DIFFICULTY

YOU WILL NEED

FABRIC:

- enough printed and plain cotton to make 59 diamonds for the front; 7 x 12cm (2¾ x 4¼in) per diamond. Divide the fabrics any way you like; I have split mine as follows: 21, 19 and 19 per print/colour
- chambray or other plain cotton for the back and lining, 50 x 100cm (19¾ x 39½in)

ADDITIONAL ITEMS:

- children's wooden clothes hanger
- 2.5cm (1in) wide cotton bias binding, 2.5m (2¾yd) long
- template, see page 193
- pattern paper, tracing wheel and curved ruler
- chalk or other erasable fabric marker
- paper for 59 diamond shapes

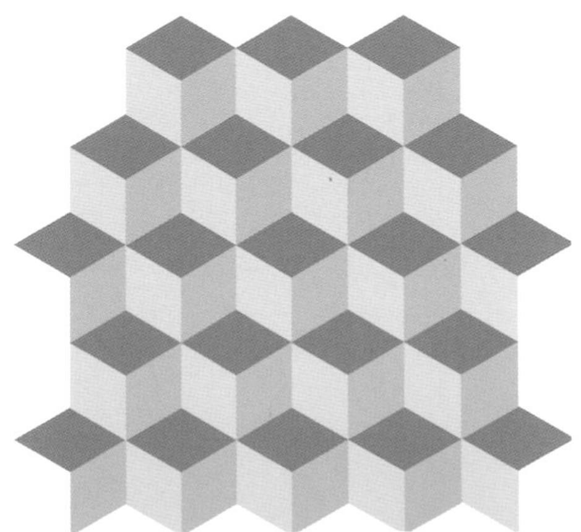

Peg Bag

1 To start, construct a pattern for the peg bag. Draw a vertical line 45cm (18in) long on some pattern paper. From the top of this line measure down about 5cm (2in) and mark a horizontal line through the vertical line (to create a cross); also mark a horizontal at the bottom of your vertical line. Take your hanger and place it directly onto the cross; place the hook onto the central line, with the base of the hook on the upper horizontal line. Draw around the hanger and place it to one side. Draw a line down from the tip of each hanger arm to meet the lower horizontal. You should now be looking at a rectangle with a hanger shape at the top. Use the natural contours of the hanger as a guide and draw in the shape of the peg bag. The sides are best drawn freehand and then neatened with a curved ruler later. Add in the peg bag opening with two curved lines. The first should start about 8cm (3¼in) from the top of the hanger; draw from the central line out towards the sides. Leave a gap of 8cm (3¼in) before drawing the second, mirrored curve in the same way. The lines should overlap at the sides (refer to the photograph, opposite).

2 Add another curved line at the top of the peg bag to allow the hanger through. Fold the paper in half along the central line and use a tracing wheel to transfer the lines from one side to the other – to check your pattern is symmetrical. Unfold and redraw the tracing-wheel lines if necessary. Add a 1cm (½in) seam allowance around all lines. With your pattern complete, trace off one full copy for the back; for the front you will need two pieces – one from the top edge to the top curve, and the other from the bottom curve down to the bottom edge. Cut and place to one side.

3 Make up your 59 paper-pieced diamonds (see pages 24–25). Using the pattern diagram, left, arrange the diamonds and stitch together using a whip stitch. This pattern is called 'tumbling blocks'.

4 Remove the tacking/basting threads and papers. Press with an iron and pressing cloth. Using chalk or a fabric marker pen, mark out the two front sections onto the tumbling blocks and the same again in backing fabric. Cut out and place the corresponding pieces together with wrong sides facing. Pin to secure, matching all raw edges.

5 Use the full peg bag pattern to cut two back sections from the chambray fabric; place them wrong sides together and pin.

6 Finish the curves at the bag and hanger openings with bias binding (see page 21).

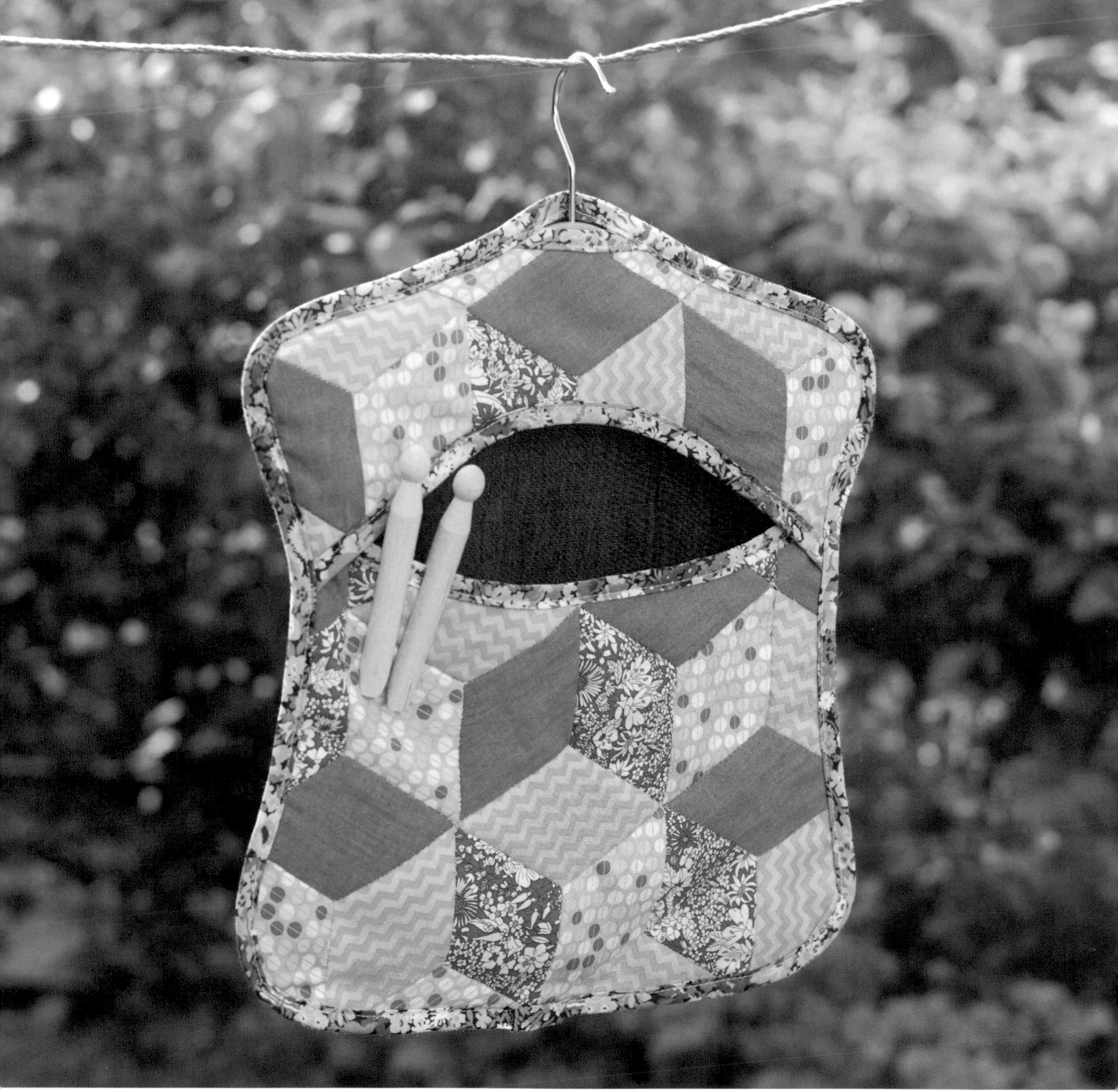

7 Layer up the bag starting with the backing, followed by the larger lower front section and then the smaller upper front section on top. Match all the raw edges around the perimeter to align. Pin to secure.

8 Finish by binding the whole bag (see page 21); start and finish on the bottom edge.

SIZE: 45 x 52CM (17¾ x 20½IN), PLUS TIES

LEVEL OF DIFFICULTY

YOU WILL NEED

FABRIC:

- natural-coloured linen for the apron, 60 x 110cm (24 x 43in)
- printed cotton for the pockets and ties, 50 x 110cm (20 x 43in)

ADDITIONAL ITEMS:

- template, see page 196
- water-soluble marker pen

CUTTING OUT

The following measurements include a 6mm (¼in) seam allowance:

- 2 pieces of linen, 47 x 54cm (18½ x 21½in), for the front and lining
- 2 pieces of printed cotton, 9.5 x 80.5cm (3¾ x 31¾in), for the ties
- 2 pieces of printed cotton, 15 x 30cm (6 x 12in), for the pockets

Scalloped Apron

1 Mark across the long bottom edges of the front and lining pieces of linen using the scallop template on page 196. Cut along the drawn lines on each piece.

2 For the ties, fold each of the fabric strips in half lengthways, right sides facing, and stitch along the long side and one end. Turn the right way out and press. On the front of the apron, position the unstitched end of each tie on a side edge, about 6mm (¼in) from the top, matching the raw edges. Tack/baste or pin in place, then ensure the ties are pinned in place on the apron front to prevent them getting caught in the seams in the following step.

3 Pin then stitch the two linen pieces together with right sides facing; leave a turning gap in one side edge. Trim the seam allowance on the scalloping, snipping up to the stitching at the points but being careful not to cut the stitching. Turn the right way out and press, then sew up the turning gap by hand.

4 Fold the pockets in half widthways, right sides facing and sew the open edges together, leaving a turning gap in one side. Turn each pocket the right way out, then press and sew up the turning gap by hand.

5 Place the pockets on the apron, 11cm (4½in) from the top and 8cm (3¼in) in from each side edge. Edge stitch the sides and bottom, stitching close to the edge of the fabric. Reinforce the stitching at the top by back-tacking a few times.

SIZE: 22 x 16CM (8¾ x 6¼IN)

LEVEL OF DIFFICULTY

YOU WILL NEED

FABRIC:

- white cotton, 34 x 17cm (13½ x 7in)
- patterned fabric scraps, at least 4.5cm (1¾in) wide
- striped fabric for binding, 6.5 x 90cm (2½ x 35½in)

WADDING/BATTING:

- fusible fleece, 22.5 x 16.5cm (9 x 6½in)

ADDITIONAL ITEMS:

- red rickrack braid, 50cm (20in)
- white crocheted lace, 20cm (8in)
- water-soluble marker pen
- white embroidery thread/floss (optional)

CUTTING OUT

The following measurements include a 6mm (¼in) seam allowance:

- 16 x 10.5cm (6¼ x 4⅛in) white cotton for the front
- 22.5 x 16.5cm (9 x 6½in) white cotton for the back
- 2 pieces of patterned fabric 4.5 x 10.5cm (1¾ x 4⅛in) for the side borders
- patterned fabric scraps, 4.5cm (1¾in) wide
- 6.5 x 90cm (2½ x 35½in) striped fabric for binding
- 22.5 x 16.5cm (9 x 6½in) wadding/batting

Good Morning Mug Rug

1 Attach the side border strips to the white fabric, with right sides facing. Sew the white crochet lace over the seams just sewn, as shown in the photograph. Tack/baste the rickrack braid about 6mm (¼in) in from the top and bottom edges.

2 Join together 4.5cm (1¾in) wide strips of patterned fabric in different lengths, then trim to make two pieces 4.5 x 22cm (1¾ x 8¾in). Sew the strips to the top and bottom of the front piece.

3 Iron the wadding/batting onto the back rectangle. Pin the front and back pieces together, wrong sides facing. With white thread, hand-embroider blanket stitch along the pieced strips, adjacent to the braid.

4 Trim the mug rug to 22 x 16cm (8¾ x 6¼in). Trim with the striped binding (see page 21).

Opposite

By Renate Bieber.

Why not embroider a greeting such as 'Good Morning' across the middle of the mug rug? This should be done before step 1. Choose a computer font you like for the wording, print out with a font size of about 100pt and then transfer the letters to the white fabric using a water-soluble marker pen. Lower the machine feed dogs and fit a darning or free-motion embroidery foot to your machine. Place embroidery stabilizer underneath the letters and sew around them using a small zigzag stitch (stitch width about 1.5). Wipe off the pen marks using a damp cloth and leave to dry. Tear off the embroidery stabilizer, then make up as given above.

français
internet

SIZE: 20 x 12 x 12CM (7¾ x 4¾ x 4¾IN)

LEVEL OF DIFFICULTY

Floral Sewing Box

YOU WILL NEED

FABRIC:

- turquoise cotton with roses for the outer, 50 x 45cm (20 x 18in)
- pink cotton lining, 50 x 45cm (20 x 18in)

WADDING/BATTING AND INTERFACING:

- 50 x 45cm (20 x 18in) double-sided iron-on wadding/batting
- 50 x 45cm (20 x 18in) lightweight iron-on interfacing

ADDITIONAL ITEMS:

- pink spotted bias binding, 125cm (49¼in)
- pink checked bias binding, 125cm (49¼in)
- cotton cord for the piping, 4mm (⅛in) diameter and 125cm (49¼in) long
- pink rickrack braid, 50cm (20in)
- 1 turquoise zip, 45cm (18in) long
- pink webbing, 20cm (8in)
- 2 pink crocheted flowers
- pink cord, 20cm (8in)
- 1 small wooden cotton reel
- 1cm (½in) wide pink elastic, 50cm (20in)
- water-soluble marker pen
- pattern paper, pencil ruler and mug

CUTTING OUT

FROM THE TURQUOISE FABRIC, CUT OUT:

- 1 piece 42 x 25cm (16½ x 9¾in), for the top/bottom
- 1 piece 50 x 20cm (19¾ x 7¾in), for the sides

FROM THE PINK FABRIC, CUT OUT:

- 1 piece 42 x 25cm (16½ x 9¾in), for the top/bottom
- 1 piece 50 x 20cm (19¾ x 7¾in), for the sides

FROM THE WADDING/BATTING, CUT OUT:

- 1 piece 42 x 25cm (16½ x 9¾in)
- 1 piece 50 x 20cm (20 x 8in)

FROM THE LIGHTWEIGHT INTERFACING, CUT OUT:

- 1 piece 42 x 25cm (16¼ x 9¾in)
- 1 piece 50 x 20cm (20 x 8in)

1 First create your templates. For the top/bottom piece, draw a rectangle 36 x 20cm (14¼ x 8in) on your pattern paper and mark the centre points of each side. Round off the four corners with the aid of a mug that is about 8cm (3¼in) in diameter.

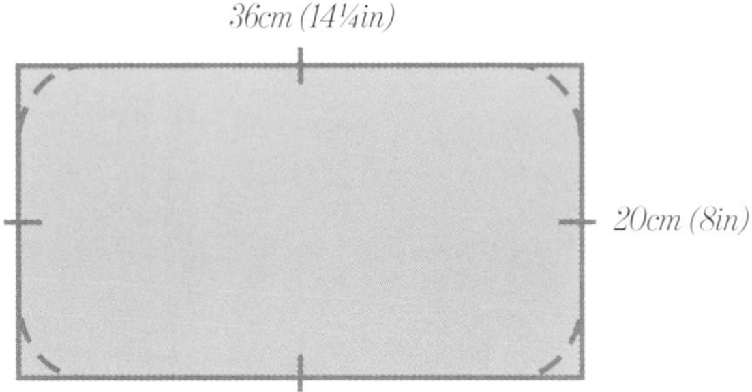

2 For the side piece, draw a rectangle 44 x 12cm (17¼ x 4¾in), mark the centres of the sides and round off the corners in the same way. Draw a line across, 4cm (1½in) from the upper edge, for the zip. Cut out both patterns.

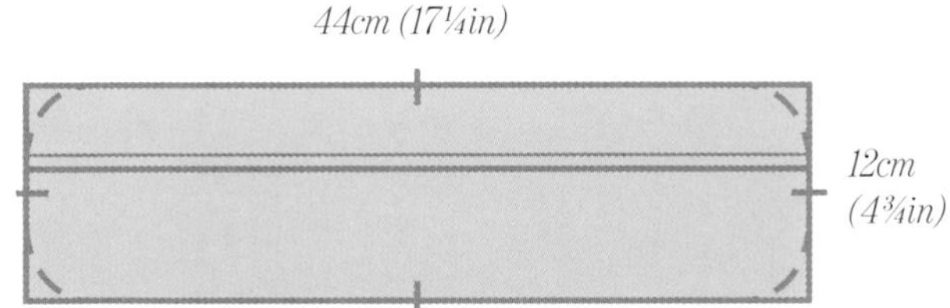

Continued overleaf...

Instructions for making the tape measure cover are on page 154.

Leinennähmaschinenzwirn
Extra prima Qualität
POLYESTER

3 For the top/bottom of the box, place the pink fabric piece wrong side up in front of you. Place the interfacing (fusible side down) on top, then the wadding/batting, and lastly the turquoise fabric, right side up. Cover the layers with a damp cloth and iron them together. Repeat the process with the side pieces.

4 On the right sides of both pieces, draw two intersecting lines at 45 degrees to the edge. Stitch along both lines with a straight stitch (stitch length 3). With the aid of a quilting ruler, stitch parallel lines 4cm (1½in) apart to cover the whole surface (see below); alternatively, see tip box right.

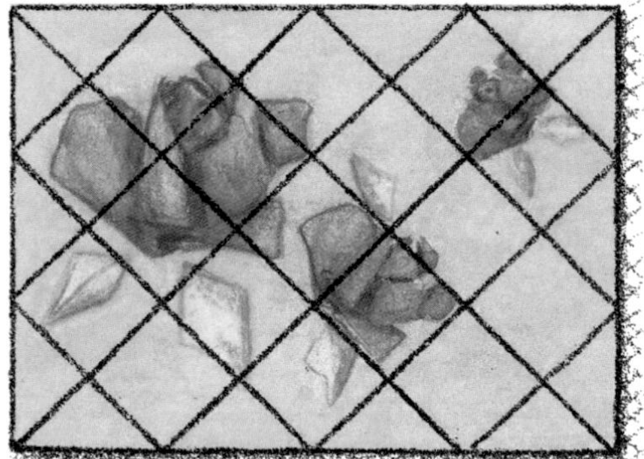

Tip

If your sewing machine does not have a quilting ruler, draw the lines on the fabric with water-soluble marker.

5 Cut across the side piece 7cm (2¾in) from the upper edge, then insert the zip (see page 26).

6 Place the paper patterns on the back of both fabric pieces, line up the position of the zip and transfer the centre point markings, then cut the fabric pieces to size, adding a 1cm (½in) seam allowance all round. Sew on the rickrack braid 2cm (¾in) below the zip.

7 For the piping, iron open the pink spotted bias binding and trim the whole length to a width of 3cm (1¼in). Make the piping with the cotton cord (see page 27). Sew the piping around the edge of the top/bottom of the sewing box, taking care to stitch just inside the seam allowance.

8 Open the zip. Pin the side piece to the top/bottom, with right sides facing, matching the marks, then sew together. Trim the seam allowance to 6mm (¼in), then sew the checked bias binding over the seam allowance by hand to cover it.

9 Fold in the ends of the webbing by about 2cm (¾in) and stitch to the top of the box to make a handle. Sew on the crocheted flowers. Thread the pink cord through the zip pull, thread both ends through the cotton reel and knot the ends together. Sew the elastic to the inside at the level of the rickrack braid, to make loops to hold your sewing notions.

SIZE: 26 x 26 x 26CM (10¼ x 10¼ x 10¼IN)

LEVEL OF DIFFICULTY

Door Stop

YOU WILL NEED

FABRIC:

- enough assorted cotton prints to cut 36 half-hexagons; 6 x 11cm (2⅜ x 4¼in) per half-hexagon
- matching fabric and felt for the base, 26 x 30cm (10¼ x 11¾in)

ADDITIONAL ITEMS:

- paper, card and paper clips
- chalk or water-soluble fabric marker pen
- cotton webbing tape, 25 x 2.5cm (9¾ x 1in)
- plastic beans
- toy stuffing
- knitting needle
- template, see page 196

1 Start by making up 36 paper-pieced half-hexagons (see pages 24–25). Join three half-hexagons to make a small triangle; use a whip stitch and sew the shapes together with right sides facing (as in diagram A). Continue to make the triangles in this way. Once you have completed four triangles, sew them together with whip stitch to form a large triangle (as in diagram B). Repeat to create a further two large triangles (see diagram C).

2 Make a base template from card by tracing around the edge of one large triangle. Cut the template out. Using chalk or a fabric marker, draw out one triangle onto the felt and another onto the desired base fabric (mark both on the wrong side of the fabric). Using fabric scissors, cut the felt triangle out along the marked lines. Now cut the base fabric out; however, this time cut 1cm (½in) outside the chalked line. This will form the seam allowance to enable the fabric to be tacked/basted onto the felt base. Place the felt triangle centrally onto the fabric base (make sure the right side of the fabric is face down) and fold over the seam allowance towards the centre of the felt. Use paper clips to secure it in place temporarily. Tack/baste the fabric onto the felt to create the base section using thick thread. Remove the paper clips.

3 Now you are ready to assemble the doorstop. Fold the webbing in half to make a loop for the handle. On one patchworked triangle, place both raw ends of the webbing along one of the long straight edges, 8cm (3¼in) down from the tip. Allow at least 1.5cm (½in) to overhang; the loop should point towards the centre of the work. Pin to secure.

4 With right sides facing, place another large triangle onto the first, matching all the points and sandwiching the handle in between. Attach these two sections using whip stitch along one edge. As you are sewing you will meet the webbing – at this point, switch to a small running stitch to secure the tape, catching both outer edges of the work and sewing through the webbing. Reverse your stitching to create a solid stitch line, which will attach the tape securely.

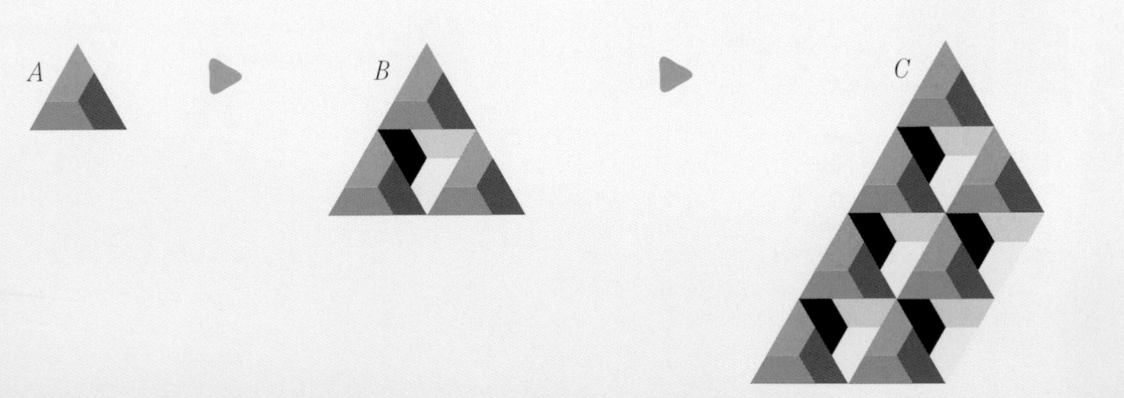

5 Attach the third triangle to create a pyramid shape, using whip stitch. You are now ready to attach the base. Turn the pyramid inside out, then pin the base piece to the bottom edges, right sides facing, making sure you match the points of the triangles. Whip stitch two of the edges together. Make sure you are catching the felt as well as the outer base fabric. This will help keep the felt in position when finished. Whip stitch the last edge but this time leave an opening 10cm (4in) wide to allow filling. Remove all of the tacking/basting stitches and papers from the doorstop. Turn right side out and tease out the points using a knitting needle.

6 Fill the top of the pyramid with toy stuffing to approximately a third of the volume and fill the rest with plastic beans.

7 Once you have a plump doorstop, close the opening using whip stitch.

Patchwork Placemats

SIZE: 30 x 40CM (12 x 16IN)

LEVEL OF DIFFICULTY

YOU WILL NEED

FABRIC FOR ONE PLACEMAT:

- natural-coloured linen, 41.5 x 64cm (16½ x 25in)
- 9 different-sized scraps of printed cotton

WADDING/BATTING:

- lightweight, iron-on fleece, 35 x 45cm (13¾ x 17¾in)

CUTTING OUT

The following measurements include a 6mm (¼in) seam allowance:

- 2 pieces of natural-coloured linen, 32 x 41.5cm (12½ x 16½in), for the front and back
- trim the edges of the printed cotton scraps as desired, e.g. straight or with pinking shears

1 To make the front, iron the wadding/batting to the wrong side of one linen rectangle. Arrange the trimmed fabric remnants on top of the linen, then sew in place with straight or zigzag stitches.

2 Place the other piece of linen on top with the right sides facing and sew together on all sides, leaving a turning gap in one edge.

3 Turn the placemat right side out, then press and hand-sew the turning gap closed. Make other placemats in the same way.

Tip

Use thermal wadding/batting instead of standard fleece in your mats to help protect your surfaces from heat damage.

SIZE: 22 x 14CM (8½ x 5½IN)

LEVEL OF DIFFICULTY

YOU WILL NEED

FABRIC:

- enough assorted cotton prints to make 28 diamonds; 8 x 12cm (3⅛ x 4¼in) per diamond
- lining fabric, 26 x 33cm (10¼ x 13in)

ADDITIONAL ITEMS:

- paper for making templates
- closed-end zip, 25cm (10in)
- cotton bias binding, 60cm (24in) long and 2.5cm (1in) wide
- chalk or water-soluble marker pen
- rotary cutter and cutting mat
- ruler
- knitting needle
- template, see page 200

Diamond Make-up Bag

1 Cut out the fabric and paper shapes and make up 28 paper-pieced diamonds. Using the pattern in the diagram below, sew them together using whip stitch; instructions for paper piecing are on pages 24–25.

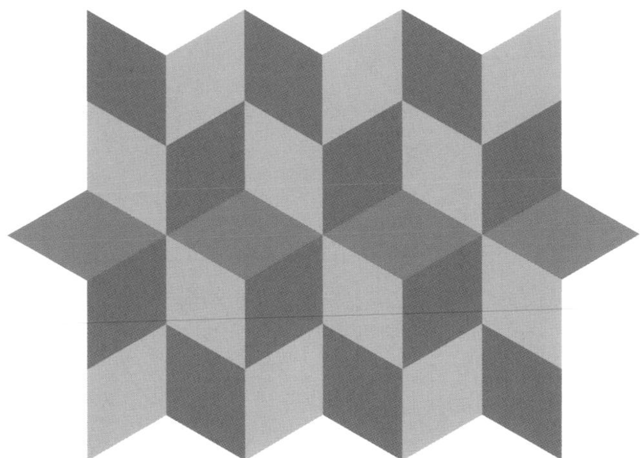

2 Remove the tacking/basting threads and the papers from the back of each shape. Press flat with a steam iron and pressing cloth. Lay the lining fabric onto the patchwork piece and mark out the edges with chalk or a fabric marker. Use a rotary cutter to cut the patchwork piece to the same shape to make the outer bag. Place the lining fabric in a portrait layout, right side up. Fold the bottom towards the top, right sides facing, matching all the raw edges. With a sewing machine, stitch the side seams closed, 1cm (½in) away from the raw edge. Repeat with the bag outer.

3 Now create the 3D shape of the bag. With an iron, press the bag outer completely flat. This will press a crease along the central line at the base of the bag. Create a boxed base corner, 4cm (1½in) along the seam (see page 16). Repeat this step on the other side of the bag and on the bottom corners of the lining.

Continued overleaf...

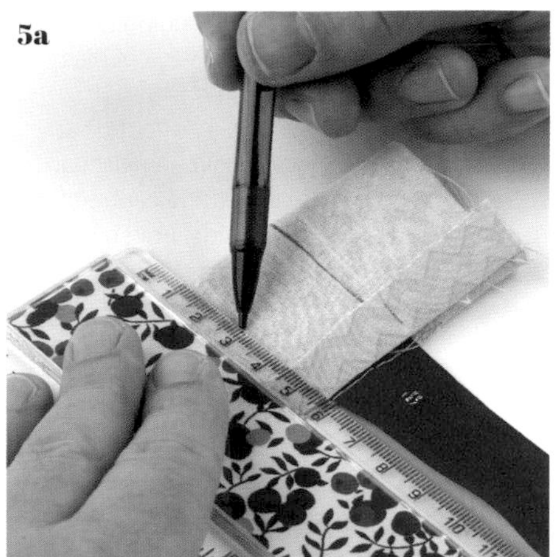

5a

5b

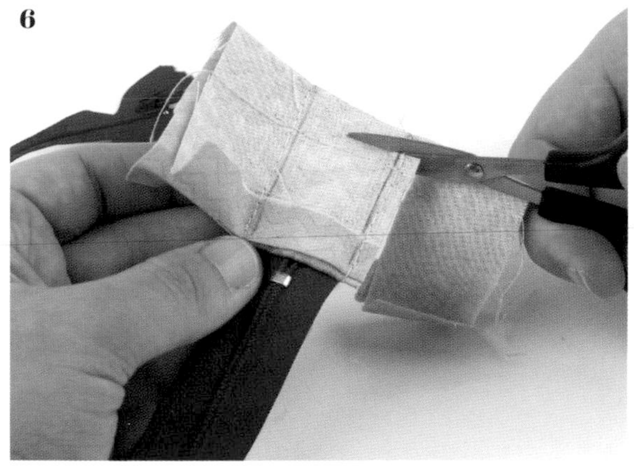

6

7

4 Now make a tab to decorate the end of the zip. Mark and cut out a rectangle of fabric measuring 4.5 x 9cm (1¾ x 3½in). Press under a 1cm (½in) seam allowance along both 4.5cm (1¾in) edges.

5 With right sides facing, fold the rectangle over so the pressed edges meet. Insert the end of the zip into the tab so that the zip stop sits just outside the tab. Draw lines along, but just outside, the sides and end of the zip tape. Stitch along these drawn lines.

6 Snip off the excess fabric around the sides and across the top of the tab.

7 Turn the tab through and tease out the corners using a knitting needle. Insert the end of the zip and hand-sew along the pressed edges, trapping the end of the zip within.

8 Turn the bag outer right side out and insert the lining with wrong sides facing. Match the side seams and pin. Machine sew around the rim of the bag. Open up the zip and pin to either side of the bag lining along the rim. The zip start and finishing point should be 2cm (¾in) away from the side-seam stitch lines. At the start of the zip, fold the zip end at a right angle towards the rim. This will finish the front of the zip and allow the ends to be hidden. Machine stitch the zip to hold in place and remove the pins. Allow the zip to run free from the 2.5cm (1in) finish point.

9 Trim the bag rim with bias binding (see page 21). First, add a small piece of bias tape measuring 4cm (1½in) in length to create a tab, which will help hide the cut edges of the bias binding when finished. Start and finish the tape at the centre of the tab, in the centre of one side. Fold over the tab to the reverse and hand stitch to finish.

SIZE: ABOUT 10 x 9CM (4 x 3½IN)

LEVEL OF DIFFICULTY

Happy Heart

YOU WILL NEED

FABRIC:

- floral cotton, 34 x 15cm (13½ x 6in)
- matching felt, 10 x 8cm (4 x 3¼in)

ADDITIONAL ITEMS:

- embroidery thread/floss in a contrasting colour to the felt
- ribbon, 25cm (10in) long
- 4 wooden buttons
- a small amount of stuffing
- templates, see page 195

1 Fold the floral fabric in half, right sides together, and pin on the larger template. Cut out to create two identical pieces. Pin the smaller template to the felt and cut out.

2 To create the pocket, position the felt heart on the right side of one fabric heart and pin it in place. Using the contrasting embroidery thread/floss, stitch the felt heart to the fabric heart with running stitch. Start at point B and continue down and around to point A. At this point, continue stitching, but through the felt layer only and not through the fabric. Continue to the end and knot.

3 Place the two fabric hearts right sides together and pin. Sew them together with a 1cm (½in) seam allowance, leaving a 5cm (2in) gap for turning through. Remember to back-tack at the beginning and end of the stitch line. Clip the curves and the point of the heart. Turn through and roll the seams gently to create a rounded shape.

4 Stuff the heart with small pieces of stuffing and hand sew the opening closed.

5 Position the ribbon at the top of the heart (as shown in the photograph) and sew the ends in place. Sew buttons over the top of the ribbon on the front and back of the heart.

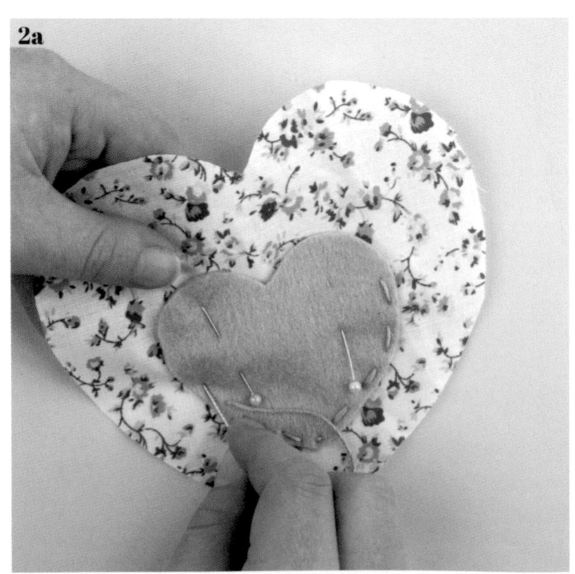

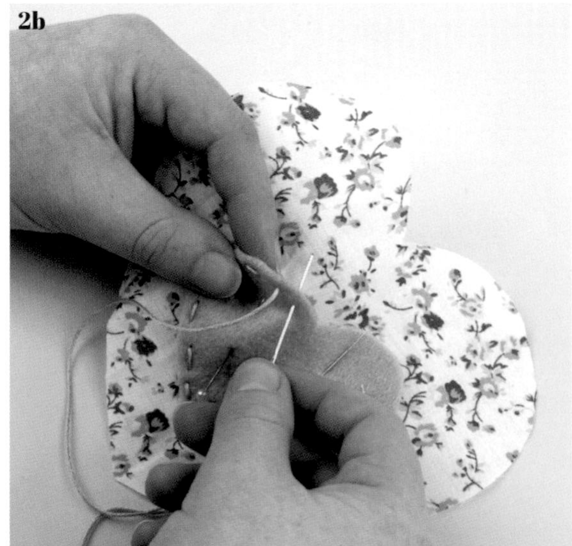

SIZE: ABOUT 32 x 20CM (12½ x 8IN)

LEVEL OF DIFFICULTY

Horse Hanger

YOU WILL NEED

FABRIC:

- red wool felt, 28 x 46cm (11 x 18in/fat eighth)
- white wool felt, 28 x 46cm (11 x 18in/fat eighth)
- blue wool felt, 28 x 46cm (11 x 18in/fat eighth)

ADDITIONAL ITEMS:

- a small amount of stuffing
- a few interesting beads – think plain, unfinished wooden and brightly coloured glass or wood; include a yellow one for the flower centre
- strong thread
- red perle no. 8 cotton embroidery thread/floss
- large plain silver hoop to hang decoration
- black and white bakers' string/twine for the saddle girth and bridle
- fabric glue stick
- templates, see page 197

1 From the red felt, cut out the horse's body, three teardrop shapes and a 23cm (9in) square. Put this square to the side for now; you will use it later for backing the horse. From the white felt, cut out the saddle pieces.

2 Glue the saddle and the accessories onto the horse: the teardrops onto the saddle and the saddle onto the body of the horse. The thinner bridle and the girth on the saddle are made from bakers' twine; glue these onto the head and hand sew a couple of anchoring stitches from the back to secure them.

3 With the red perle cotton thread/floss, embroider around the edges of the saddle with a running stitch.

4 Lay the embellished horse onto the untrimmed red square and pin. Machine sew around the edge, leaving a small gap somewhere inconspicuous. Stuff the horse shape with polyester stuffing and then close the gap. Trim the felt back.

5 From blue felt, cut out the heart shape and a 15cm (6in) square for the backing; cut the individual petals for the daisy from the white felt.

6 Glue the white petals onto the heart, and then attach the yellow bead to the centre. Finish the heart in the same way as you did for the horse (see step 4).

7 Thread a needle with a long length of the strong thread and attach it to the top of the heart. Thread your beads onto it in a pleasing pattern and then anchor the other end to the bottom middle of the horse's belly.

8 Thread up again and, this time, anchor the strong thread in the middle of the horse's back. Add beads again, and finish with your silver hanging hoop at the top.

Tip

Don't over-stuff the heart and the horse. Just a little is needed to give them some shape.

Tip

When you slide on the top beaded thread, check to see that the horse is balanced. Simply hold it up by the thread and if it tips to the side, alter the thread position.

SIZE: 29 x 19 x 12CM (11½ x 7½ x 4¾IN)

LEVEL OF DIFFICULTY

YOU WILL NEED

FABRIC:

- spotty outer fabric, 50 x 60cm (20 x 24in)
- geometric lining, 50 x 60cm (20 x 24in)

WADDING/BATTING:

- fusible foam, 50 x 60cm (20 x 24in)

CUTTING OUT

FROM THE OUTER FABRIC, CUT OUT:

- 2 rectangles for the top and bottom, 30 x 20cm (12 x 8in)
- 1 strip for the upper zipped panel, 58.5 x 4cm (23 x 1½in)
- 1 strip for the lower zipped panel, 58.5 x 9cm (23 x 3½in)
- 1 piece for the back panel, 30 x 13cm (12 x 5in)

FROM THE LINING, CUT OUT:

- 2 pieces for the top and bottom, 30 x 20cm (12 x 8in)
- 1 strip for the upper zipped panel, 58.5 x 4cm (23 x 1½in)
- 1 strip for the lower zipped panel, 58.5 x 9cm (23 x 3½in)
- 1 piece for the back panel, 30 x 13cm (12 x 5in)
- 1 piece for the pocket, 18 x 15cm (7 x 6in)
- 1 piece for the handle, 6.5 x 23cm (2½ x 9in)

FROM THE FOAM STABILIZER, CUT OUT:

- 2 pieces for the top and bottom, 30 x 20cm (12 x 8in)
- 1 strip for the upper zipped panel, 57 x 2.5cm (22½ x 1in)
- 1 strip for the lower zipped panel, 57 x 7cm (22½ x 2¾in)
- 1 piece for the back panel, 29 x 11.5cm (11½ x 4½in)
- 1 strip for the handle, 2 x 20cm (¾ x 8in)

ADDITIONAL ITEMS:

- continuous zip, 61cm (24in)
- 30cm (12in) circle template
- repositionable fabric adhesive
- about 2m (2¼yd) of bias tape

Geometric Sewing Box

1 First, make up the pocket by folding the fabric in half to 18 x 7.5cm (7 x 3in), right sides together. Sew around the raw edges, leaving a gap in the long side of about 7.5cm (3in) for turning. Snip off the corners.

2 Turn the pocket right side out and press. Edge stitch the folded side.

3 Take the 30 x 20cm (12 x 8in) rectangles of outer and lining fabrics and the foam stabilizer, and, using your 30cm (12in) circle template, draw then cut a curve to one side of each piece.

4 Use a little repositionable spray adhesive to adhere the foam stabilizer centrally to the wrong sides of the outer fabric pieces.

4

5 To make the handle, wrap the fabric around its corresponding foam stabilizer, folding in the raw edges. Edge stitch all the way round.

6

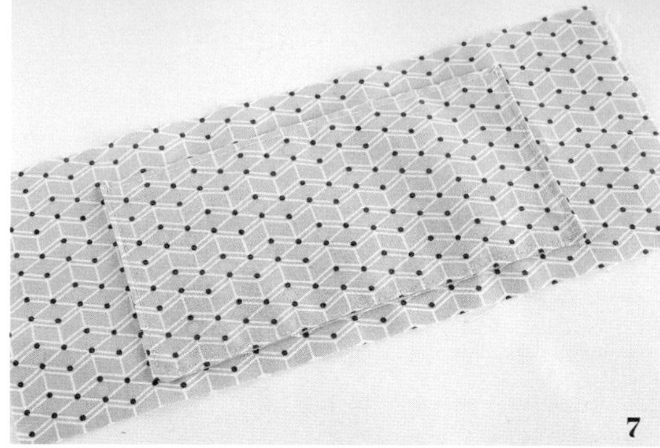
7

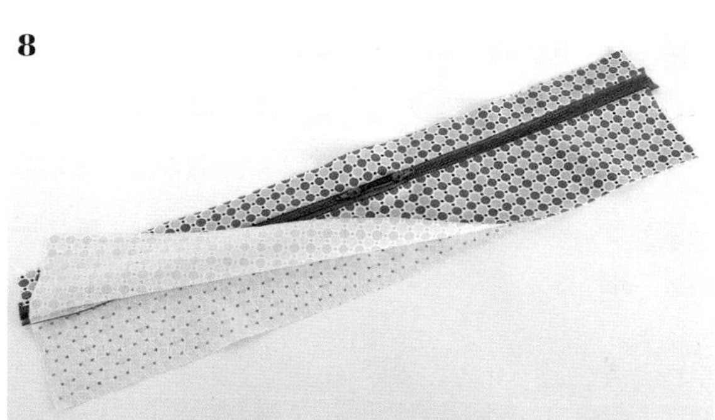
8

9

10

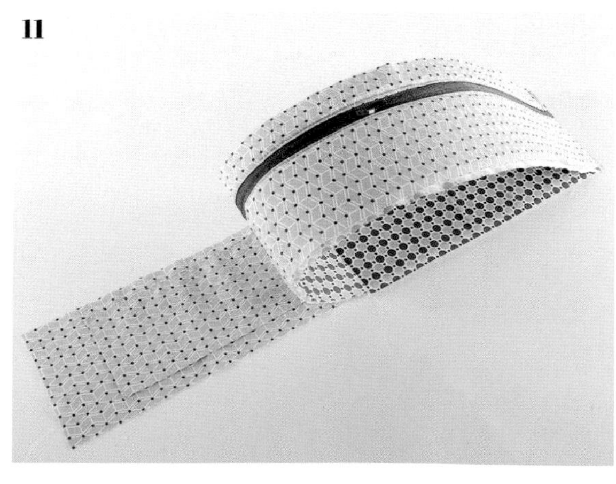
11

6 Measure and mark 7.5cm (3in) from the straight side of the top (one of your backed outer pieces created in step 4), and 7.5cm (3in) from the curved side. Use these measurements to position then sew the handle ends in place in a box shape.

7 Sew the sides and bottom of the pocket centrally to the back panel lining piece.

8 Sew the top and bottom outer zip panel pieces to either side of the zip tape, right sides together. Then sew the linings to the opposite sides. Press, then topstitch along the seams.

9 Spray one side of the zip-panel foam stabilizer pieces with repositionable adhesive and adhere them to the outer fabric, either side of the zip.

10 Spray and adhere the foam stabilizer to the outer back panel. Sew the outer back panel to the zip section, right sides together along one short end. Then sew the back lining to the same seam, right side facing the lining side of the zip panel. Press, then topstitch.

11 Fold the zipped section over so that the opposite ends meet, and sew the outer pieces right sides together.

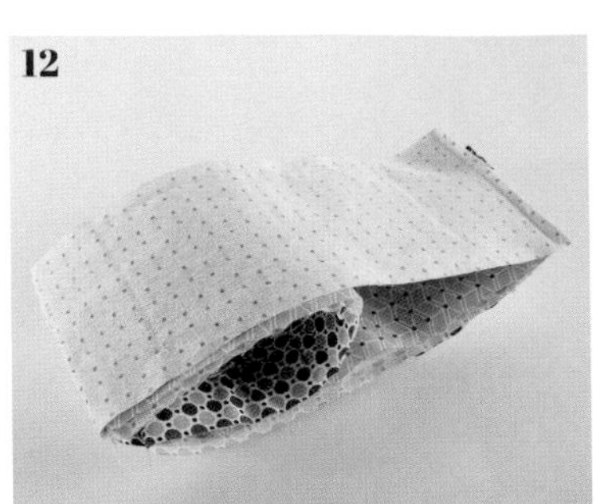

12

13

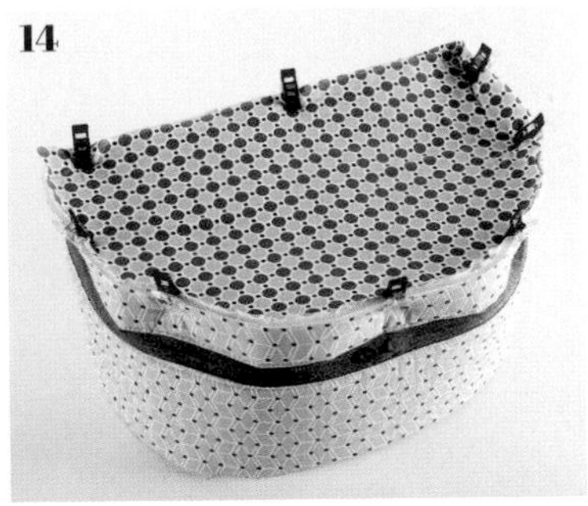

14

15

12 This next bit may seem a bit tricky – fold the lining pieces right sides together, rolling the zipped section out of the way; sew.

13 Open out this section and you'll see the shape of the case forming. Topstitch the remaining seam.

14 Turn this ring inside out. Use the adhesive spray to secure the lining to the lid and base pieces from step 4, wrong sides together. Clip the top of the case to the sides, with right sides together (this may now be too thick to pin).

15 Sew all the way round and remove the clips as you go. Apply bias tape all the way round, folding the end inwards as you start and overlapping by about 1cm (½in) when the two ends meet.

16 Fold the tape over and hand sew with slip stitch. Repeat at the base of the case.

17 Turn the case right side out and press. Fill with fabrics, scissors and threads and off you go!

SIZE: 10.5 x 19CM (4 x 7½IN)

LEVEL OF DIFFICULTY

YOU WILL NEED

FABRIC:

- red polka-dot cotton for the front and back, 20 x 60cm (7¾ x 24in)
- strawberry print cotton for the flap, 12 x 25cm (4¾ x 9¾in)
- pink polka-dot cotton for the lining, 20 x 80cm (7¾ x 31½in)

WADDING/BATTING AND INTERFACING:

- fusible wadding/batting, 20 x 60cm (7¾ x 24in)
- lightweight iron-on interfacing, 12 x 25cm (4¾ x 9¾in)

ADDITIONAL ITEMS:

- 10mm (½in) diameter press stud
- white rickrack, 50cm (20in)
- templates, see page 198

CUTTING OUT

The following measurements include a 6mm (¼in) seam allowance:

- red polka-dot cotton: 2 pieces using the main bag template
- strawberry print cotton: 1 piece using the flap template
- pink polka-dot cotton: 2 pieces using the main bag template and 1 piece using the flap template
- wadding/batting: 2 pieces using the main bag template
- interfacing: 1 piece using the flap template

Tip

For an added touch, insert a folded piece of ribbon between the outer fabrics at step 5 to create a cute ribbon tag, as shown right.

Strawberry Make-up Bag

1 For the flap, iron the interfacing onto the wrong side of the outer flap piece. Place the outer edge of the rickrack neatly around the bottom of the flap and edge stitch securely.

2 Place the flap outer and lining pieces together with right sides facing, and sew together around the curved edge. Turn right side out, press and edge stitch.

3 For the bag outer pieces, fuse a piece of wadding/batting to the back of each outer piece. Sew up the darts, right sides facing. Sew the darts in the pink polka-dot lining pieces in the same way.

4 Place a bag lining piece together with one bag outer piece, right sides facing, and edge stitch along the top, working close to the edge. Open out the fabrics, press, then edge stitch across the top again (this is the front piece).

5 For the bag back, with the right sides of the fabric facing, pin the flap to the middle of the top of the back. Then place the remaining lining piece on top of the two other layers, with the right sides facing, and sew across the top. Open out the fabrics and edge stitch across the top of the back.

6 Pin the front and back pieces together with the right sides facing, outer to outer and lining to lining, making sure the seams are matched.

7 Sew around the edge of the whole piece, but leave a turning opening of about 10cm (4in) at the bottom of the lining.

8 Turn right side out and neaten the corners. Fold the seam allowances of the turning opening to the inside. Sew up the opening, then tuck the lining to the inside.

9 Position then fit the press stud in the middle of the flap, about 6mm (¼in) above the bottom edge, and about 5cm (2in) below the top edge, referring to the manufacturer's instructions. Fit the other half of the press stud to the front of the bag.

GREENLEAF
liquid stay
Rose

SIZE: 47.5 x 31.5CM (18¾ x 12½IN)

LEVEL OF DIFFICULTY

YOU WILL NEED

Based on a cutting mat measuring 46 x 30cm (18 x 12in):

FABRIC:

- 2 pieces of geometric cotton for the outer, 53.5 x 40.5cm (21 x 16in)
- 2 pieces of spotted cotton for the lining, 53.5 x 40.5cm (21 x 16in)
- 4 pieces of cotton for the pockets: 2 plain and 2 patterned, each measuring 63.5 x 15cm (25 x 6in)

WADDING/BATTING:

- 2 pieces of fusible fleece, 53.5 x 40.5cm (21 x 16in)

ADDITIONAL ITEMS:

- magnetic clasp
- 2 lengths of 2.5cm (1in) wide webbing, each 40cm (16in)
- water-soluble fabric marker pen
- ruler

Craft Caddy

1 Fuse the fleece to the back of the outer fabric pieces. Measure 15cm (6in) down the sides and along the top from each top corner, and cut at an angle between these points. Repeat to trim the lining pieces.

2 Fold the lining pieces in half to crease the centre lines. Measure and mark 4cm (1½in) down from the top edge. Cut two 5cm (2in) squares of lining fabric from the leftover corners, and place behind your marks – this will help to strengthen the fabric around the clasp sections. Apply one half of the clasp to the right side of each lining piece at the mark.

3 To make up the first pocket, place a patterned fabric piece and plain fabric piece right sides together and sew along the long edges to make a tube. Turn right side out, and roll so that a 1cm (½in) strip of lining shows at the top. Press, then topstitch along the seam.

4 Pin the raw side edges of the pocket piece to the sides of the front of the bag, 5cm (2in) up from the base; the pocket will be larger than the bag outer, to allow space for pocket compartments.

5 Pin the pocket at intervals to make dividing pockets – these can be any size you like. If you have specific tools or equipment you'd like to store, pop them inside the pocket and place your pins around them.

6 Mark the dividing lines with your fabric marker, then sew, removing the pins. Topstitch the bottom of the pocket, folding the loose fabric into pleats as you sew. Sew the side seams. Repeat to create and attach another pocket to the back of the bag.

7 Tack/baste the webbing handles, facing inwards, to the top side of each half of the bag.

1

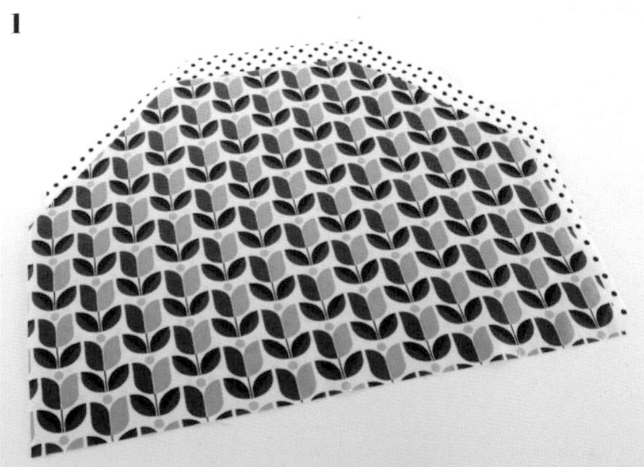

5

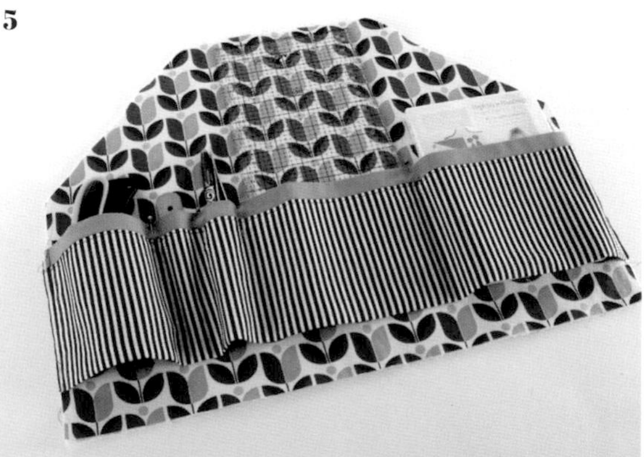

8

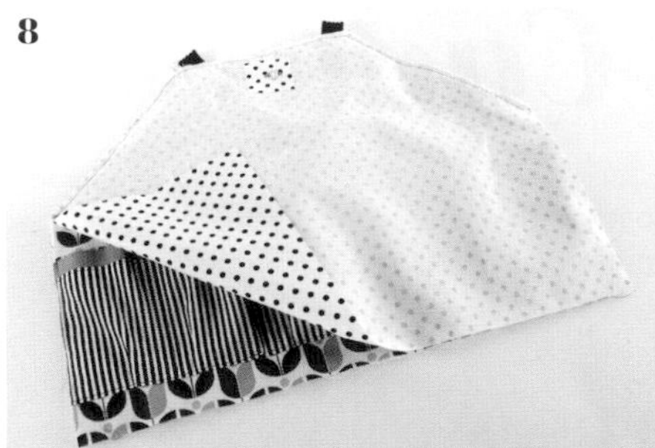

8 Place a lining piece over the front outer panel, right sides facing. Sew together along the top and sloping sides, trapping the webbing securely in place. Repeat with the back panel.

9

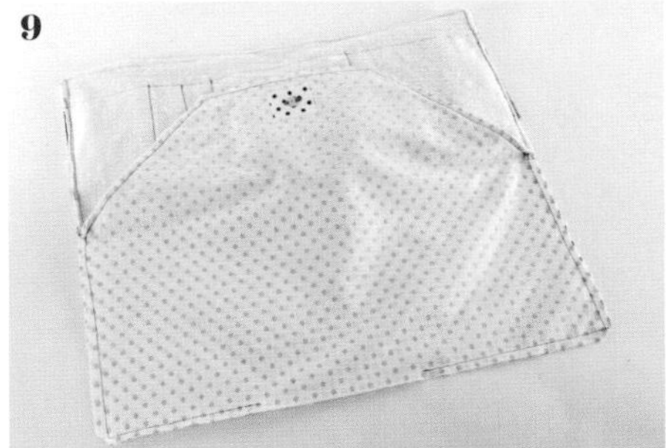

9 Sew the two pocket panels right sides together, starting and stopping at the point where the lining meets. Fold the flaps out of the way, and sew the lining pieces together in the same way, leaving a gap in the base of about 15cm (6in) for turning.

10 Turn right side out and press. Sew the opening in the lining closed then push the lining inside the bag. Press around the top then edge stitch to complete.

SIZE: 22CM (8¾IN) DIAMETER

LEVEL OF DIFFICULTY

YOU WILL NEED

FABRIC:

- striped cotton for the outer sides, 70 x 16cm (27½ x 6¼in)
- striped cotton for the outer base, 25 x 25cm (10 x 10in)
- blue dotty cotton for the lining sides, 70 x 16cm (27½ x 6¼in)
- blue dotty cotton for the base lining, 25 x 25cm (10 x 10in)

WADDING/BATTING:

- 2 pieces of fusible fleece, 70 x 16cm (27½ x 6¼in)
- 2 pieces of fusible fleece, 25 x 25cm (10 x 10in)

ADDITIONAL ITEMS:

- 1 crocheted flower in white
- 1 red bead
- water-soluble marker pen
- template, see page 200

CUTTING OUT

- To make the template for the base, fold a sheet of newspaper in half lengthways then widthways. Transfer the quarter circle template and cut out. This creates the pattern piece for the complete circle of the base. Fold the paper cut-out into four equal segments and mark the folds on the outer edge. Draw the template circle onto the back of both fabric squares and the two wadding/batting squares, including the marks, and cut out.

Bread Basket

1 To make the sides of the bread basket, iron the wadding/batting rectangles onto the back of the two fabric rectangles. With the right sides facing, sew the two short ends of the outer fabric strip together to form a circle, then press the seam allowance open. Repeat for the lining fabric, but leave about 10cm (4in) in the centre of the seam unstitched for turning. Divide these rings into four equally sized sections, and mark each section on the bottom long edge.

2 To make the base, iron the base wadding/batting circles onto the back of the base fabrics.

3 Pin then sew the outer base fabric to the outer side fabric, right sides facing and aligning the marks on the fabric. Repeat for the lining base and side pieces.

4 Place the one basket inside the other, with right sides facing, aligning the seams. Sew around the top edge. Turn right side out through the opening in the lining seam and sew the opening up by hand. Push the lining into the outer basket and fold the top edge over by about 4cm (1½in). Sew the crochet flower and bead onto the edge.

SIZE: 40 x 110CM (16 x 43¼IN)

LEVEL OF DIFFICULTY

YOU WILL NEED

FABRIC:

- assorted cottons: enough to cut 37 squares, 12.5 x 12.5cm (5 x 5in)
- 2 pieces of red and white striped cotton, 6.5 x 112cm (2½ x 44in)
- white backing fabric, 45 x 120cm (18 x 47¼in)

WADDING/BATTING:

- thin fleece, 45 x 120cm (18 x 47¼in)

ADDITIONAL ITEMS:

- red and white checked bias binding, 3.3m (3⅝yd)

Table Runner

1 Lay out the cut squares with the points upwards, alternating columns with two squares next to columns with three squares (see diagram below). Follow the photograph of the design or arrange your own fabrics any way you like.

2 Sew the squares together in diagonal rows and press, with the seam allowance of each row in alternate directions.

3 Sew the rows together. Cut off the points on all the outside edges, leaving a seam allowance of 6mm (¼in) at the tips of the inner squares (see diagram, below).

4 Cut two pieces of bias binding the length of the long sides. Iron open the folds of the bias binding, then fold each section in half lengthways, wrong sides facing, and pin. Sew together with a 6mm (¼in) seam allowance so they will not slip later.

5 Lay the bias binding along both long sides, right sides together. Place the strips of striped fabric right sides together on top, so that the stripe sequence is symmetrical at both ends.

6 Sew on the bias binding and edge strips in a single operation. Cut off any extra edging strip close to the edge. Press the seam allowances of the squares so the border of checked fabric lies on top of the edging strips.

7 Cut the wadding/batting and white backing fabric a little larger than the front. Place the front and back right sides together and stitch both to the wadding/batting along the two long sides. Trim away the wadding/batting very close to the seams and cut the backing material to the same size as the front.

8 Turn through the runner and press. Quilt around the squares by stitching in the ditch. On the short sides, cut the wadding/batting and backing to the size of the front and bind the open ends with the bias binding (see page 21).

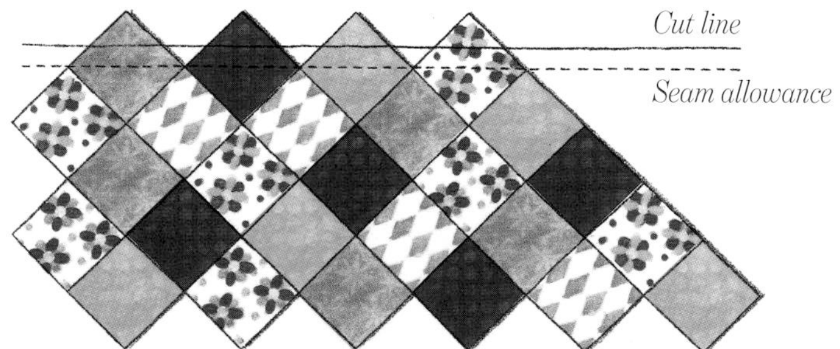

POST
CARD
13599
GREENGATE POSTAGE
COPENHAGEN DK

SIZE: 20 x 30CM (8 x 12IN), PLUS HANDLE

LEVEL OF DIFFICULTY

YOU WILL NEED

- A: spotty cotton, 45 x 83.5cm (18 x 33in)
- B: sewing notions cotton, 158 x 40cm (62 x 16in); you may have to join two pieces of fabric together in step 3, so doublecheck your fabric widths before you buy

WADDING/BATTING:

- fusible fleece, 93.5 x 20cm (37 x 8in)

ADDITIONAL ITEMS:

- ribbon, 70cm (27in) long and 1cm (½in) wide
- 10 buttons – follow the manufacturer's instructions if you want fabric-covered buttons like mine
- embroidery thread/floss
- safety pin or bodkin
- water-soluble fabric marker pen

Tidy Caddy

1 Cut two circles of fabric A for the base, each measuring 20cm (8in) across. Fuse fleece to the wrong side of one piece.

2 For the sides, cut two pieces of fabric A measuring 63.5 x 20cm (25 x 8in), and again, fuse fleece to the wrong side of one piece.

3 Cut two strips of fabric B measuring 158 x 15cm (62 x 6in) for the pockets – you may have to join two pieces together.

4 Cut one piece of fabric B measuring 20 x 10cm (8 x 4in) for the handle; cut and fuse fleece to the wrong side. Fold the long sides to the centre, then fold in half. Topstitch along both long sides.

5 Satin stitch across the two short ends of the handle.

6 Cut two pieces of fabric B, each measuring 64 x 10cm (25 x 4in), and one strip of fabric A measuring 66 x 5cm (26 x 2in) for the drawstring section. Fold the ends of fabric A over twice by 1cm (½in) and sew.

7 Fold the strip of fabric A in half lengthways, wrong sides together and press. Place the fabric B drawstring section pieces right sides together, and sandwich the folded strip of fabric A in between, with the raw edges together at the top. The folded section should be 1cm (½in) shorter at each end than the fabric B pieces.

8 Sew the three sections together across the top. Open out and press.

9 Fold the whole piece right sides together so that the short sides meet. Sew along the short end. Push one side inside the other so that the drawstring channel is at the top and press again.

Continued overleaf...

5

8

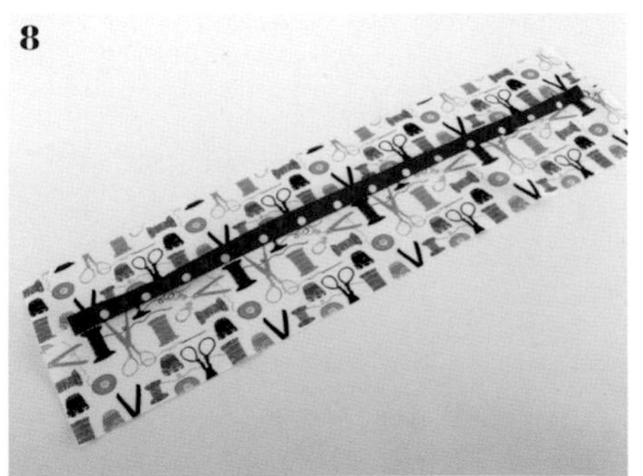

9

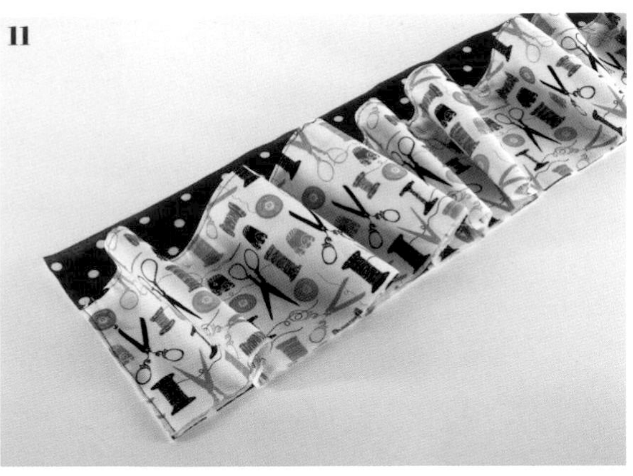
11

12

14

Tip

Use a little spray starch on the pocket fabric to help keep the creases sharp.

10 Take the two pocket pieces and sew them together across the top long edge, right sides together. Fold over so that they sit with the wrong sides together and press. Edge stitch 3mm (⅛in) from the top.

11 Fold the pocket fabric in half and crease the centre line, fold in half again and crease the quarters, then in half again and crease the eighths. Open out the fabric and mark these lines with fabric marker pen. You could measure and mark the fabric into eighths if you find that easier. Mark the side section of fabric A that you've backed with fleece in the same way. Place the pocket strip over the top of the side piece, tack/baste the sides together, then pin at the marked lines. You'll see the eight pocket shapes starting to form. Stitch 6mm (¼in) in from each side edge.

12 Stitch along each of the marked lines to divide. Remove the pins. Flatten each pocket shape and re-pin so that the folds meet – leave 1cm (½in) free at each side to allow for the seam allowance. Sew straight across the bottom of the pockets, close to the edge.

13 Remove all the pins. Fold the two short sides right sides together, making sure the pockets are tucked out of the way of your stitch line. Sew together to make a tube.

14 Sew in the circular base with the fleece backing, right sides facing. To help with fitting, fold both the tube and base into quarters and crease, then pin together at these marks before sewing. Remove the pins and turn right side out.

15 Sew a button over the dividing stitch line between each pocket – you will have two buttons left over.

16 Fold the remaining 63.5 x 20cm (25 x 8in) piece of fabric A into a tube, aligning the short ends and with the right sides facing. Sew along the short ends, leaving a gap of about 10cm (4in) for turning. Insert the remaining circular base – right sides facing in – in the same way as in step 14. This is your lining.

17

18

19

17 Keeping the lining section inside out, drop the outer pocketed section inside the lining, so that the right sides are together; line up the side seams. Insert the drawstring section between the outer and lining pieces, aligning the raw edges. Sew all the way around the top.

18 Turn right side out through the gap in the lining. Sew the opening closed by hand, then push the lining inside the caddy and press. Edge stitch around the top of the bag – you may need to use the free arm on your sewing machine.

19 Thread the ribbon through your bodkin, then feed this through the drawstring channel and pull tight. Alternatively, pin a safety pin through the end of the ribbon, and use this to help guide the ribbon through.

20 Attach the handle with the ends on opposite sides of the top of the caddy using embroidery thread/floss: take the needle from the inside of the caddy, through the handle and a button, back through the caddy and tie on the inside. Don't pull the thread too tight – the handle needs to pivot.

When you're not using the caddy, pull the drawstring tight and use the handle to carry. When you're using it, fold the handle over and undo the drawstring.

SIZE: ABOUT 13 x 35CM (5 x 13¾IN)

LEVEL OF DIFFICULTY

YOU WILL NEED

FABRIC:

- turquoise cotton with large pattern, 22 x 43cm (8¾ x 17in)
- 2 pieces of turquoise and white striped cotton, 9.5 x 43cm (3¾ x 17in)
- 2 pieces of turquoise cotton, 9.5 x 43cm (3¾ x 17in)

ADDITIONAL ITEMS:

- pink and white checked bias binding, 2 lengths of 43cm (17in)
- pink bias binding, 2 lengths of 43cm (17in)
- pink satin cord, 2 lengths of 50cm (20in) long, 4mm (⅛in) in diameter
- cotton cord for piping, 4 lengths of 43cm (17in), 4mm (⅛in) in diameter
- 1 foam bolster pad, 13 x 35cm (5 x 13¾in)
- safety pin or bodkin

Bolster Pillow

1 For the piping, iron open the folds of the bias binding. Trim to a width of 3cm (1¼in), fold in half and place the cotton cord inside. Pin in place and sew close to the cord (see page 27).

2 Sew the fabric pieces together to form a striped pattern, following the diagram below. Sew the two plain pink piping strips to the central piece and the checked piping between the other two seams. Neaten the seam edges with zigzag stitch.

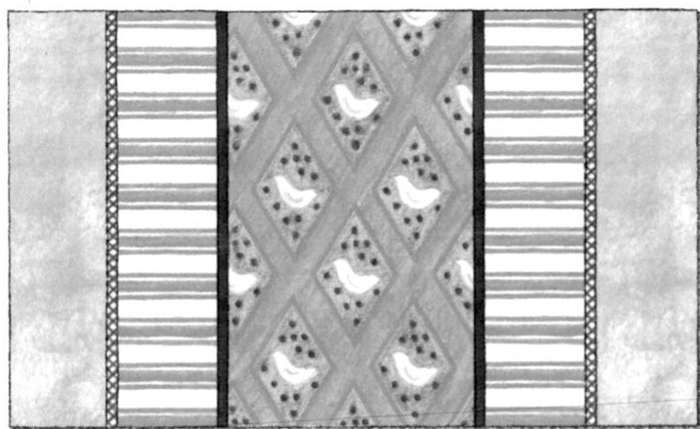

3 Fold the patchworked fabric in half, lengthwise, right sides together. Sew up the long open edges, then neaten the seam. On the two short edges, fold over a double hem of 1cm (½in). Topstitch along the edge but leave a small opening in the seam for threading the cord into the channel later. Turn through.

4 Thread the satin cord through the channels with the help of a safety pin or bodkin. Insert the bolster pad in the cover. Pull the satin cords tight and tie the ends in a bow.

SIZE: 144 x 198CM (56¾ x 78IN)

LEVEL OF DIFFICULTY

YOU WILL NEED

FABRIC:

- 88 squares of 19.5 x 19.5cm (7½ x 7½in), from at least nine different cottons
- 7 strips of striped fabric for the edging, 5 x 99cm (2 x 39in); alternatively, use 7m (7yd) of pre-pressed bias binding
- 210 x 150cm (82½ x 59in) of backing fabric

WADDING/BATTING:

- fusible fleece, 210 x 150cm (82½ x 59in)

ADDITIONAL ITEMS:

- 9 crocheted doilies, 9–14cm (3½–5½in) diameter
- small lace motifs
- 2.5cm (1in) bias tape maker (optional)

Patchwork Quilt

1 Lay out the fabric squares in eleven rows of eight, as you please. Sew the squares together in rows, and then sew the eleven rows together.

2 Cut the fleece and fabric for the back, making them a little bigger than the front piece. Put the three layers together (with the fleece between the outer two pieces, which should be wrong sides facing) and secure with tacking/basting stitches or safety pins. Quilt by stitching in the ditch. Trim the fleece and backing fabric to the same dimensions as the front.

3 Sew together all the edging strips, if using, then run through a bias tape maker (see page 20). Apply as continuous bias binding around the edge of your quilt (see page 21).

4 Arrange the crocheted doilies over the quilt and sew on by hand. Sew tiny lace motifs on at the points where the squares meet, if you like.

SIZE: 33 x 23CM (13 x 9IN)

LEVEL OF DIFFICULTY

YOU WILL NEED

For a 33 x 23cm (13 x 9in) bottle:

FABRIC:

- calico, 46 x 30.5cm (18 x 12in)
- backing cotton, 46 x 30.5cm (18 x 12in)
- lining cotton, 46 x 61cm (18 x 24in)
- 15 strips of fabric of various widths, each at least 28cm (11in) long

WADDING/BATTING:

- fleece, 46 x 61cm (18 x 24in)

ADDITIONAL ITEMS:

- ribbon, 81cm (32in), for ties
- bias binding, 1m (1yd)
- 6 strips of lace and ribbon of various widths, each at least 28cm (11in) long
- card to make a template

Hot Water Bottle Cover

1 Draw around the hot water bottle on the card, leaving a border of around 5cm (2in) all the way round. Cut out the template, then fold in half lengthways to make sure it is symmetrical. Use to cut one shape from the calico, one from the fabric for the back and two from the lining fabric.

2 Take the first strip of fabric and lay it right side up across the bottom of the calico. Place the second strip right side down, overlapping the first at a slight angle, and sew across the top (2a). Flip the second strip right side up and press. Repeat until all the calico is covered (2b).

Continued overleaf...

2a

2b

3 Stitch strips of ribbon or lace across some of the seams. Don't use scratchy lace – you want a super-snuggly cover! Embellish each side of the seams, using a decorative stitch if you like.

4 Place this piece of the hot water bottle cover right side up on top of one piece of wadding/batting. Lay the fabric for the back right side down on top, then finally the second piece of wadding/batting.

5 Sew together, from just below the curve of the 'shoulder', round the bottom and up to the same point on the other shoulder, leaving the top open to slip the hot water bottle inside. Trim the excess fabric back to the shape of the calico.

6 Place the lining fabrics right sides together and sew in the same way. Leave the lining inside out.

7 Turn the outer cover the right way out. Push the lining into it.

6

8 Cut the ribbon into four, then pin each piece facing inwards to the neck of the cover on the front and back.

8

9 Sew the bias binding around the opening, trapping the ribbon in the stitching (see page 21). Put the filled hot water bottle inside then tie the ribbons to secure.

9

SIZE: 6 x 7CM (2½ x 2¾IN)

LEVEL OF DIFFICULTY

YOU WILL NEED

FABRIC:

- multicoloured cotton, 10 x 19cm (4 x 7½in)
- red spotted cotton, 20 x 24cm (8 x 9½in)

WADDING/BATTING:

- fleece, 10 x 19cm (4 x 7½in)

ADDITIONAL ITEMS:

- scrap of green felt
- pink pompom braid, 30cm (12in)
- pink cord, 30cm (12in)
- 1 flower-shaped button
- 1 self-winding tape measure
- fabric glue
- ruler
- water-soluble marker pen
- template, see page 199

CUTTING OUT

FROM THE RED SPOTTED FABRIC, CUT OUT:

- 2 pieces 4 x 9cm (1½ x 3½in)
- 2 pieces 4 x 11cm (1½ x 4¼in)
- 1 piece 10 x 19cm (4 x 7½in)

NOTE:

These instructions refer to the house with the red roof.

Tip

If you cut the template from transparent film it will be easier to see the grain of the fabric and to position it accurately.

Tape Measure Cover

1 Draw around the template for the house on the back of the multicoloured cotton and cut out, adding a 6mm (¼in) seam allowance. Transfer the markings on the template onto the fabric. Place the shorter 4 x 9cm (1½ x 3½in) red strips of the sloping roof on the top left and bottom right sections of the multicoloured patterned fabric.

2 Pin in place and sew along the markings on the pattern. Fold the strips over and press with a dry iron. Extend the markings for the sloping roof onto the back of these strips with the aid of a ruler.

3 Sew the longer 4 x 11cm (1½ x 4¼in) red strips along this line, right sides together, and iron open. On the wrong side of the fabric trace the template for the house plus roof and cut out, adding a seam allowance.

4 Place this, right sides together, on the 10 x 19cm (4 x 7½in) piece of red spotted fabric and place both on the piece of wadding/batting. Sew all around with a small stitch (stitch length 2), leaving an opening for turning. Trim the wadding/batting close to the seam and cut the backing fabric to the size of the front. Trim away the seam allowance at the corners. Turn the house right side out and sew up the opening by hand.

5 Topstitch the seams between the roof and the house. Attach the pompom braid along the edges of the roof, leaving a little extra braid at each end. Fold this extra to the back and stitch on by hand.

6 Fold the house in half, wrong sides facing, and sew up both side edges with invisible stitches. Insert the tape measure, pull a little of the tape out, then sew up the edges of the sloping roof.

7 For decoration, draw around a coin on the felt and cut out. Sew the button to the felt. Glue the circle to the house at the point where the push-button is located on the tape measure, if it has one. Make a hole in the tape measure just below the metal tab, with a thick needle, or cut one with a sharp pair of scissors. Thread the pink cord through the hole and knot the ends together. Fold up the bottom corners of the house and sew in place with a few hand stitches.

SIZE: ABOUT 19 x 14CM (7½ x 5½IN)

LEVEL OF DIFFICULTY

YOU WILL NEED

FABRIC:

- 2 pieces of natural linen for the front and back, 20.5 x 15cm (8 x 6in)
- 1 piece of patterned natural linen for the outer pocket, 30 x 15cm (11¾ x 6in), plus a scrap for covering the button (optional)
- white cotton for the lining, 45 x 17cm (17¾ x 6¾in)

WADDING/BATTING:

- medium iron-on volume fleece, 45 x 17cm (17¾ x 6¾in)

ADDITIONAL ITEMS:

- white piping, 15cm (6in)
- elastic cord, 2mm (⅛in) diameter, 15cm (6in)
- 1 button to cover, 2cm (¾in) diameter

NOTE:

The cover is suitable for tablets or eReaders measuring a maximum of 17.2 x 12 x 1cm (7 x 4¾ x ⅜in).

For all other devices, calculate the dimensions as follows:

height + thickness + ease + 1.5cm (½in) seam allowance = height

width + thickness + ease + 1cm (⅜in) seam allowance = width

Tablet Case

1 Fold the outer pocket fabric into a square with the wrong sides facing and press. Sew the piping onto the inside of the fabric fold. Place the pocket onto the right side of the front fabric, matching the bottom edges, then tack/baste along the bottom edge to secure. Place the back fabric on top with the right side facing down. Stitch all the layers together along the bottom edge, then neaten the seam allowance with zigzag stitch.

2 Turn the pieces out. Edge stitch along the bottom edge of the pocket (through the pocket and front fabric only) then pin the pocket to the front to hold it in place.

3 For the lining, open out the case, and cut the lining and fleece to the same size. Fold the lining in half across the middle and cut along the fold (to make a front and back). Iron the opened-out front/back outer fabric onto the adhesive side of the fleece. Fold the elastic cord into a loop and sew the ends to the middle of the bottom edge (which will be the top back edge of the completed case) using zigzag stitch – the loop faces in towards the fabric. Place the lining pieces over the top and bottom sections of the bag with the right sides facing, and stitch together along the shorter top and bottom edges only.

4 Place the front and back together with the right sides facing – outer to outer and lining to lining. Make sure that all the seams are placed together neatly. Sew all around the bag, leaving a turning opening of about 7cm (2¾in) at the bottom of the lining.

5 Trim the corner seam allowances at an angle. Turn the bag right side out, and carefully neaten the corners. Fold the seam allowance of the turning opening to the inside. Machine sew the open seam and tuck the lining inside the case.

6 Cover the button with the scrap of fabric in accordance with the manufacturer's instructions, and sew onto the case by hand, making sure the loop can fit snugly around it.

Ausgeschaltet
JEANNETTE WALLS
Autorin des Bestsellers »Schloss aus Glas«
Ein ungezähmtes Leben

SIZE: 35 x 40CM (13¾ x 15¾IN)

LEVEL OF DIFFICULTY

YOU WILL NEED

FABRIC:

- blue checked cotton, 55 x 60cm (21¾ x 23½in)
- fabric scraps in blue and white

WADDING/BATTING:

- 2 pieces of fusible fleece, 30 x 35cm (12 x 14in)

ADDITIONAL ITEMS:

- white lace, 60cm (23½in)
- 1 picture frame, with a 25 x 30cm (9¾ x 11¾in) opening
- textile adhesive

Jewellery Pinboard

1 Remove the back from the picture frame and set it aside. Attach the two pieces of fleece to each other with a little adhesive, and then stick both to the front side of the picture frame back. Trim it flush against the outer edges. Fold the cotton around the frame back; stretch the fabric tight and secure the long edges with long lacing stitches. Do the same along the short edges.

2 Cut the lace into two equal-sized pieces. Pin to the fabric and sew on by hand using tiny stitches. Fit the covered back into the picture frame and secure.

3 To make the yo-yos, cut three circles out of the scraps of fabric measuring 5, 7 and 10cm (2, 2¾ and 4in) diameter. Fold the outer edge of the circles approximately 6mm (¼in) in to the wrong side of the fabric. With a needle and knotted thread, hand-sew along the fabric fold in running stitch. When you are back at the starting point, gently pull the thread to gather the circle (see illustration, below). Secure the end of the thread with a backstitch and glue the yo-yos onto the pinboard.

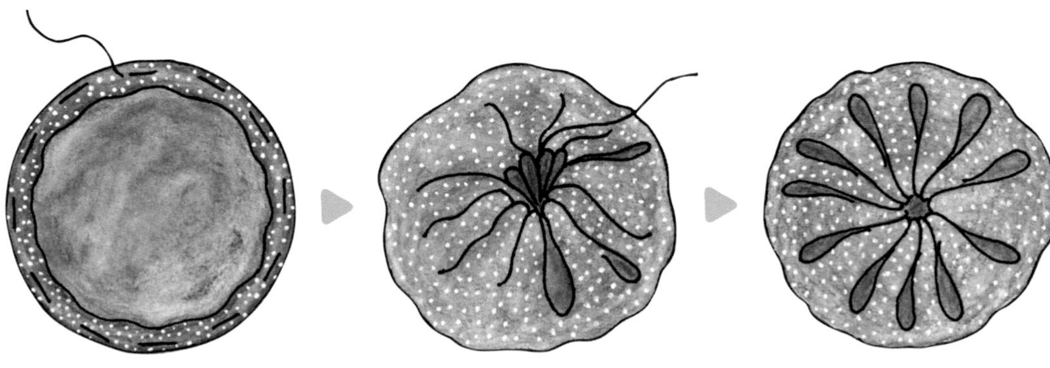

natural kids

SIZE: ABOUT 9 x 9CM (3½ x 3½IN)

LEVEL OF DIFFICULTY

YOU WILL NEED

FABRIC FOR ONE EGG COSY:

- multicoloured fabric with large spots for the upper outer, 25 x 8cm (10 x 3¼in)
- 1 piece of spotty turquoise fabric for the lower outer, 25 x 4.5cm (10 x 2in)
- 2 pieces of spotty turquoise fabric for the lining, 10 x 10cm (4 x 4in)

WADDING/BATTING FOR ONE EGG COSY:

- 25 x 12cm (10 x 5in) iron-on wadding/batting

ADDITIONAL ITEMS FOR ONE EGG COSY:

- red and pink checked bias binding, 25cm (10in)
- miniature pompom
- water-soluble marker
- template, see page 199

Egg Cosies

1 Iron the bias binding flat and cut back to a width of 2.5cm (1in). Fold in half lengthways and fasten with pins. Place the two outer strips of fabric right sides together with the bias binding in between them and the raw edges matching. Sew the strips and binding together in one operation.

2 Iron the seam allowances towards the multicoloured fabric with the large spots. Cut the wadding/batting to the same size and iron it on to the wrong side. Topstitch along the seam between the binding and the large-spotted fabric with long stitches. Draw the template pattern twice on the wadding/batting with the water-soluble marker; the dotted line will lie on the seam between the two strips of fabric. Cut all the way around, adding a 6mm (¼in) seam allowance.

3 To make the lining, draw around the pattern on each turquoise fabric square. When cutting out, only add a seam allowance to the curves; do not add a seam allowance to the bottom edge. This means the lining will be slightly smaller and will fit better inside the egg cosy.

4 Sew each egg cosy outer piece to a piece of lining along the straight edges.

5 Place the two parts right sides together, lining to lining and outer to outer, and sew all the way around, leaving a small opening for turning in the lining. Clip the seam allowance on the curves, close to the seam.

6 Turn through, sew up the opening and push the lining to the inside. Sew on the pompom by hand.

SIZE: 10CM (4IN) DIAMETER

LEVEL OF DIFFICULTY Ⅰ

YOU WILL NEED

FABRIC:

- pink polka-dot cotton, 15 x 30cm (6 x 12in)
- rose-print cotton, 15 x 30cm (6 x 12in)
- cream polka-dot cotton, 10 x 20cm (4 x 8in)
- pink felt for the rose, 2 x 20cm (¾ x 8in)
- beige felt scraps for the leaves

ADDITIONAL ITEMS:

- white rickrack, 35cm (14in)
- synthetic stuffing
- 1 reel of extra-strong thread in dusky pink
- textile adhesive
- templates, see page 202

Triple Layer Cake

1 Transfer the circular patterns to the back of the fabrics – cut two circles from each with a 6mm (¼in) seam allowance.

2 For each tier of the cake, place the two fabric circles together with the right sides facing, and sew all around with small stitches (stitch length 1.5–2). Trim the seam allowance back. Make a small cut in the middle of one of the fabric layers for turning. Turn right side out, then stuff and sew up the opening by hand.

3 Cut a length of extra-strong thread measuring about 2m (79in). Thread a needle and knot the ends so you are using it double. Mark the middle of the back of each tier. From there, push the needle up through the cushion to the top. Work once all the way around the outside, returning to the middle of the back and pushing the needle through the top again. Work the needle around the outside a total of six times in this way to make six equally sized segments. Be sure to pull the thread tight every time and secure it on the back. Work all three pieces in the same way.

4 Glue the rickrack around the bottom piece using the textile adhesive. Glue the three layers of the cake together.

5 To make the rose, roll the felt strip up a little bit, working from one narrow end. After 2–3cm (¾–1¼in), turn the strip over and continue rolling loosely, holding the curled shape in position at the base with your fingers. Turn the strip once more and continue rolling until you have rolled the entire strip into the shape of a rose. Sew through the bottom of the rose to keep it in shape. Cut two leaves from the beige felt using the template, then sew on top of the cake. Glue the rose to the top of the cake with a little textile adhesive.

SIZE: 15 x 10CM (6 x 4IN)

LEVEL OF DIFFICULTY

YOU WILL NEED

FABRIC:

- matryoshka patterned cotton for the front/back, 33.5 x 16cm (13½ x 6½in)
- dusky pink cotton for the lining, 33.5 x 16cm (13½ x 6½in)

ADDITIONAL ITEMS:

- green elastic, 1cm (½in) wide and approximately 37cm (14½in) long

NOTE:

These dimensions will fit an A6 (4 x 6in) notepad, 18mm (about ¾in) thick. If your notepad is different, adjust the measurements accordingly. Place the book on the fabric and fold the fabric over the cover; the fabric fold should measure 5cm (2in). Add a total of 1cm (½in) seam allowance and 6mm (¼in) for ease.

Book Cover

1 Lay the outer fabric down, right side up; the short edges are the sides. Cut a piece of elastic measuring about 18.5cm (7¼in) and sew to the top and bottom edges 7.5cm (3in) from the left-hand edge. The elastic should protrude beyond the edges by about 1cm (½in).

2 Cut a piece of elastic measuring 15cm (6in) for the pen holder, and fold in half. Pin the loop centrally to the left-hand side edge of the outer fabric. The elastic loop should point inwards beyond the planned folded edge by about 6mm (¼in). Sew the ends of the elastic in place, leaving a gap of 1.5cm (¾in) – this is where the pen will go.

3 With the right sides facing, pin the outer and lining fabrics together and sew all round, taking a 6mm (¼in) seam and leaving a turning opening of about 5cm (2in) at the bottom. Turn the cover right side out. Carefully push out the corners, and press. Turn the seam allowances of the turning opening to the inside and pin.

4 Turn the left and right side edges over by 4.75cm (1¾in) and pin. Check to make sure the book will fit. There should be a little give along the side edges. When you are happy with the fit, edge stitch along all sides; this will also close the turning opening. Sew over the folded sections three times. Make sure that the elastic closure is on the back, and take care not to sew over the pen holder.

SIZE: ABOUT 7–10CM (2¾–4IN) DIAMETER

LEVEL OF DIFFICULTY

YOU WILL NEED

FABRIC:

- print patterned cotton, 15 x 30cm (6 x 12in)

ADDITIONAL ITEMS:

- small baking tin or cutter
- stuffing
- textile adhesive
- hot glue gun
- decorations such as lace, tiny roses, beads, lace motifs
- pencil and cardboard

MAKING A TEMPLATE

- To make the template, turn the baking tin or cutter upside down on a piece of thin cardboard and draw round the outside. Draw a 6mm (¼in) seam allowance all round. Cut out along the outer contour, and use this as a template for the pincushion.

Vintage Pincushion

1 Use your template to draw out two circles and cut them out from the cotton. Place them right sides together and sew all around with tiny stitches (stitch length 2).

2 Snip into the seam allowance on the curves. Make a small cut in the centre of one of the fabric circles for turning. Turn through, then stuff and sew up the opening.

3 Apply some hot glue from the glue gun into the bottom of the baking tin and push the fabric cushion into the tin. If you are using a cutter, push the cushion into the cutter and secure it from underneath with hot glue.

4 You can decorate the pincushion in a number of ways, perhaps by putting lace around the tin and tying it into a bow, or sticking on lace motifs and roses with textile adhesive. To make the frill between the pincushion and tin, use a darning needle to push the lace into the gap, and secure it in a few places with hot glue. If you are using a tin with wavy sides, you can sew a bead into each groove to decorate the outside.

DRUCKKNOPF
Art. 300
CR
RC
1/2 Dtz.

SIZE: EACH STOCKING 14 x 20CM (5½ x 8IN)

LEVEL OF DIFFICULTY

Stockings Advent Calendar

YOU WILL NEED

FABRIC:

- 12 pieces of felt in two colours, 22 x 32cm (9 x 12½in)
- 12 pieces of fabric in two colours/designs, 22 x 32cm (9 x 12½in)

ADDITIONAL ITEMS:

- fusible web
- a selection of trimmings of your choice: rickrack, felt offcuts, ribbon
- pegs
- ribbon or twine for hanging
- pinking shears (optional)
- templates, see page 201

1 Take each of the felt pieces and fold it in half, right sides together. Using the template, cut out 12 pairs of the mini stocking, six in each colour. Repeat with the fabric pieces, so you have 24 stocking pairs in total.

2 For the fabric appliqué: iron fusible web onto the reverse of the appliqué fabric leftovers, draw on a motif or cut out an image from the design of the fabric, remove the backing and iron on to the background fabric. Sew round the motif.

3 Cut a variety of motifs from the leftover felt, using your imagination. There is no need to use fusible web for the felt appliqué, as felt is a quite a stable fabric. Simply pin and stitch the felt pieces in place. You can also trace the toe and heel from the template or sew strips of felt or fabric, layered with rickrack or ribbon across the stocking, about 6cm (2⅜in) from the top.

4 To construct the fabric stockings: pin two stocking pieces right sides together and sew around with a 1cm (⅜in) seam allowance, leaving the top open. Trim the seam allowance with pinking shears. Turn over 2cm (¾in) at the top and sew round the top of the stocking 1cm (⅜in) from the edge. Turn the stocking through.

5 To construct the felt stockings, follow the instructions for the fabric stockings. Alternatively, create a fold-over cuff by turning the stocking through and folding 2cm (¾in) over to the right side. Trim into a zigzag shape with scissors if desired.

6 Display the mini stockings, attached with pegs on a length of ribbon or twine. You can add numbers to the pegs if you wish, printed or stamped onto card.

3

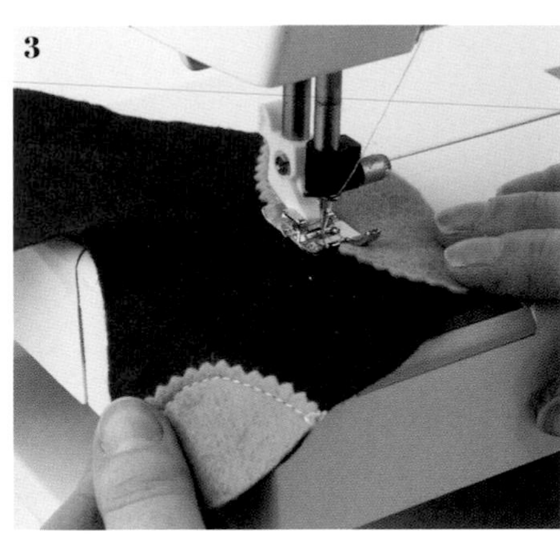

5

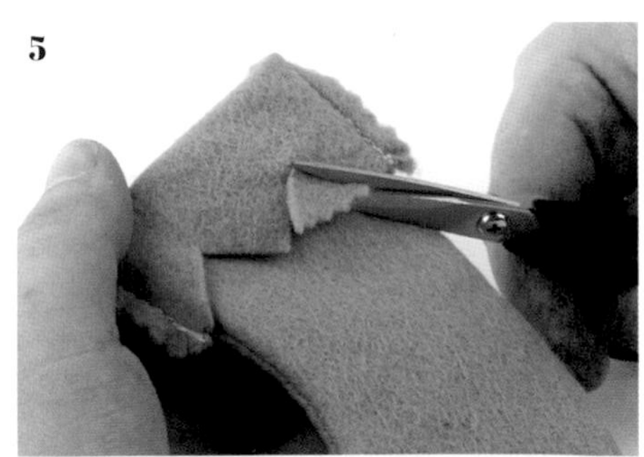

2
3
4
5
6
7
8
13
14
15
16
17
18
19

SIZE: 8 x 10CM (3¼ x 4IN)

LEVEL OF DIFFICULTY

YOU WILL NEED

FABRIC:

- 2 circles of fabric measuring 13cm (5in) in diameter
- 2 circles of fabric measuring 15cm (6in) in diameter

ADDITIONAL ITEMS:

- about 75g (2¾oz) of toy stuffing
- embroidery thread/floss
- lace, 50cm (½yd) long and 4cm (1½in) wide
- ribbon, 50cm (½yd) long and 1cm (½in) wide
- 10cm (4in) string of beads
- 1 button
- long needle – mine measures 13cm (5in)
- embroidery needle
- water-soluble fabric marker pen and quilting ruler
- pinking shears (optional)

1

2

Pumpkin Pincushion

1 Take one large and one small circle – these will be the top of the bottom section and the bottom of the top section – and cut a slit in the centre of each, 5cm (2in) long. Hand or machine sew over the ends of each cut to stop them ripping when you come to stuff the pincushion. If you have a bar tack stitch on your machine, this is perfect!

2 Take the large cut circle from step 1, and the uncut small circle. On the right side, divide each into six segments using a fabric marker pen and the 60-degree line on your ruler.

3 Sew the large and small circles right sides together in pairs, then snip all the way round with pinking shears. If you don't have any pinking shears, make small 'v' shaped cuts into the seam allowance, avoiding the stitches. This will help the seam to sit flat.

4 Turn each circle right side out through the slit you made in the centre.

5 Stuff each piece tightly, then oversew the openings closed by hand. Don't worry about being too neat here – you won't see the stitches when the pincushion is put together.

Continued overleaf...

5

6

6 Take a piece of embroidery thread/floss, about 76cm (30in) long, thread it onto your long needle and tie a large knot about 10cm (4in) from the end. Push your needle down through the centre of one of the stuffed circles, bring it up following one of the lines you've marked, and take it back through the centre. Pull tight and repeat until you have divided your cushion into six segments. Tie the two ends of the thread, knot them and trim the ends, then do the same with the second stuffed piece to create your two 'pumpkins'.

7

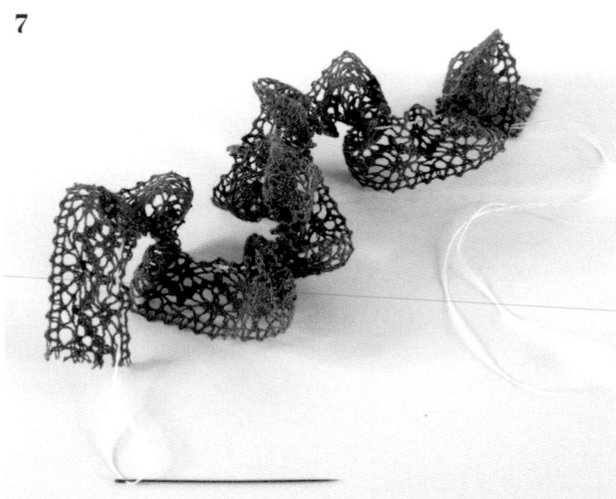

7 Using a length of embroidery thread/floss and your embroidery needle, take running stitches through one long edge of the lace to gather it. Leave the ends loose to make tying easier.

8 Gather a 30cm (12in) length of ribbon in the same way, but this time pull together and tie to make a little rosette (see finished piece, opposite, for reference).

9 Place the small pumpkin on top of the large one with the slitted sides meeting in the centre. With embroidery thread/floss and your long needle, sew straight down through the centre of both. Take the needle and thread it through a button, placed on the bottom of the pincushion. Take the needle back through the other hole in the button, through the pumpkins...

10 ...and up through the rosette on the top. Tie the thread off to secure it.

11 Tie the gathered lace around the middle of the pincushion and knot. Make a bow from the remaining ribbon and sew to one side, along with the string of beads.

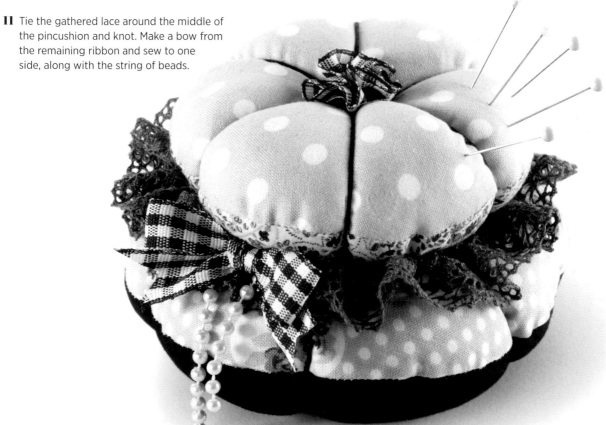

SIZE: 8 x 19CM (3¼ x 7½IN)

LEVEL OF DIFFICULTY

YOU WILL NEED

FABRIC:

- A: tulip pattern cotton for the front/back, 15 x 50cm (6 x 20in)
- B: striped cotton for the lining, 15 x 50cm (6 x 20in)

WADDING/BATTING:

- C: medium iron-on fleece, 15 x 50cm (6 x 20in)

ADDITIONAL ITEMS:

- 1 heart shaped eyeglass or metal purse frame, 5 x 17cm (2 x 6¾in)
- textile adhesive
- pliers and a piece of felt or fabric
- template, see page 202

CUTTING OUT

The pattern includes 6mm (¼in) seam allowance. Cut the pattern on the fabric fold.

- A: 2 glasses cases
- B: 2 glasses cases
- C: 2 glasses cases

Glasses Case

1 Iron the wrong sides of the two pieces of fabric A onto the two pieces of fleece. Place the two pieces of fabric A together with the right sides facing and sew the bottom edge between the marks * (see template). Sew together the lining pieces in the same way, but leave them wrong sides facing out.

2 Place the lining inside the outer with the wrong sides facing. Iron well along the top edges, and edge stitch around the top of the two sections as close to the edge as you can.

3 Drip textile adhesive into one channel of the purse frame. Be careful not to use too much or it will leak out and leave a mess on the fabric. Push the back of the case into the frame, starting in the middle. Use a fork or something similarly flat and blunt to help.

4 Use pliers to squeeze the two bottom ends of the frame onto the fabric. Put a piece of felt or fabric between the pliers and the metal so you don't scratch the frame. Don't squeeze too hard as you will mark the metal. Check to make sure that fabrics A and B are both well positioned in the frame.

5 Repeat for the front. Leave the case open for about 24 hours. Use a little water and a piece of fabric to rub off any leftover adhesive on the frame. You will not be able to do this later on.

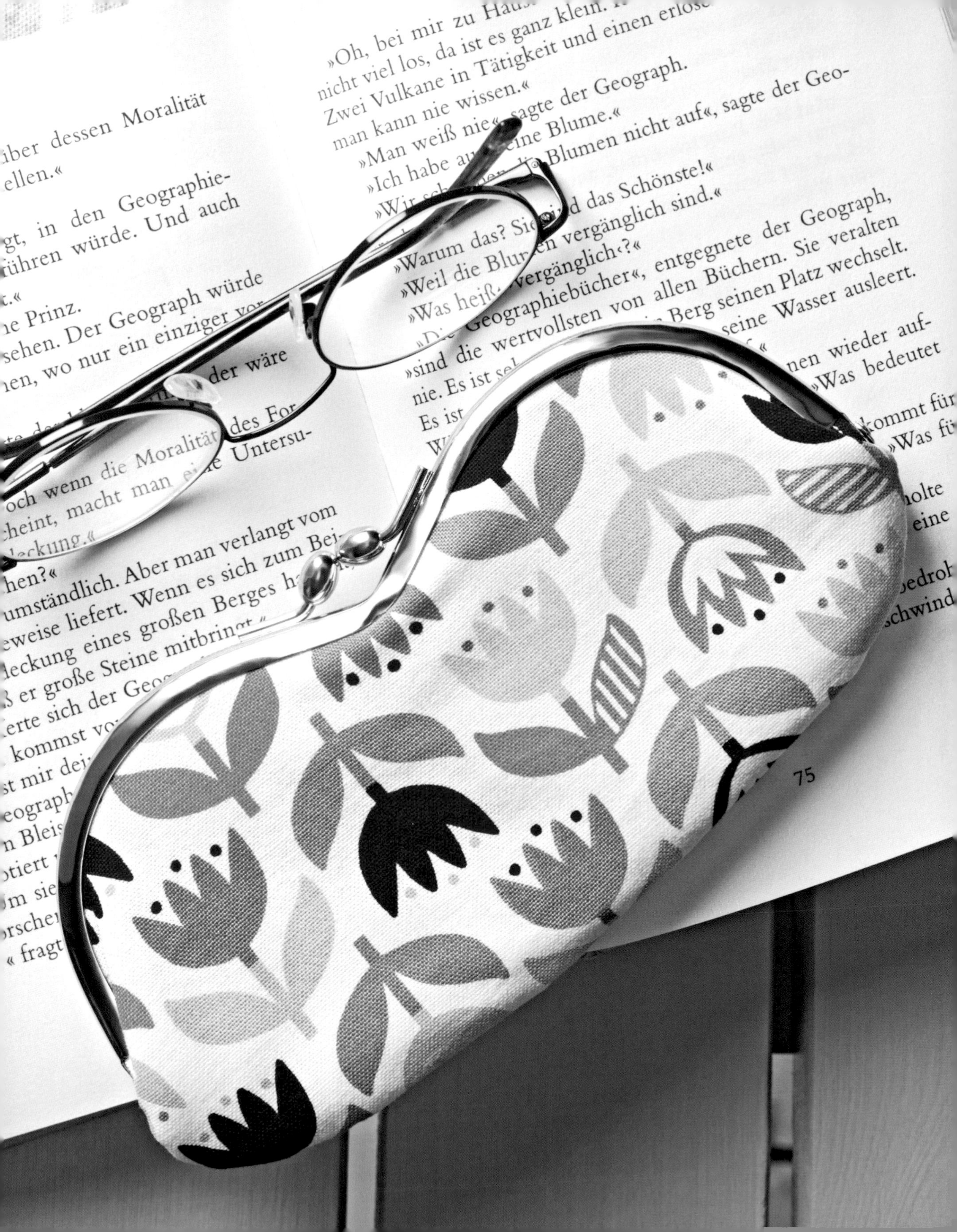

SIZE: 28 x 34CM (11 x 13½IN)

LEVEL OF DIFFICULTY

Appliqué Trees Stocking

YOU WILL NEED

FABRIC:

- outer fabric, 41 x 66cm (16 x 26in)
- lining fabric, 41 x 66cm (16 x 26in)
- felt for hanging loop, 3 x 15cm (1¼ x 6in)
- assorted cotton and felt scraps for trees
- cotton for grass, 35 x 20cm (13¾ x 8in)

ADDITIONAL ITEMS:

- fusible web
- card, pen and an adult sock
- rickrack, ribbon and embroidery threads/floss
- tree templates, see pages 204–205
- large piece of card and a pencil

1 To start with, create your stocking template. Place the adult sock onto the card and draw around it, adding about 5cm (2in) all around to create a pleasing shape, plus an extra 10cm (4in) at the top. Cut it out.

2 Take the outer fabric and fold it in half, right sides together, then pin on and cut out the template. Repeat for the lining fabric.

3 Take the fusible web and iron it onto the reverse of your chosen tree fabrics. Use the templates to cut out five or six trees. Cut a freehand curve from the grass fabric and sew it in place at the bottom of the stocking front. Machine stitch wavy lines over the grass, catching green and gold embroidery threads/floss as you sew.

4 Take your fabric trees, remove the backing paper and arrange on the stocking front. Iron them in place and machine stitch around the edges to secure them. At this point you can also add rickrack, ribbon or embroidery-thread details for extra interest.

5 To make the hanging loop, fold the felt in half lengthwise, then place a length of rickrack over the top and sew it all together, close to the edge.

6 Place the front of the stocking and the corresponding lining piece right sides together and pin then sew along the top edge. Repeat for the back of the stocking. Press the seams down towards the outer fabric.

7 Pin the front and back pieces together, lining to lining and outer to outer, matching the seams and trapping the hanging loop between the front and back layers. Sew round the stocking, remembering to leave a gap in the lining big enough to fit your hand through. Back-tack at the beginning and end of the seam line.

8 Clip the curves and turn the stocking the right way out. Push all the curves into shape. Hand sew the opening in the lining closed. Push the lining into the stocking, making sure to push it fully into the toe. Press to finish.

3

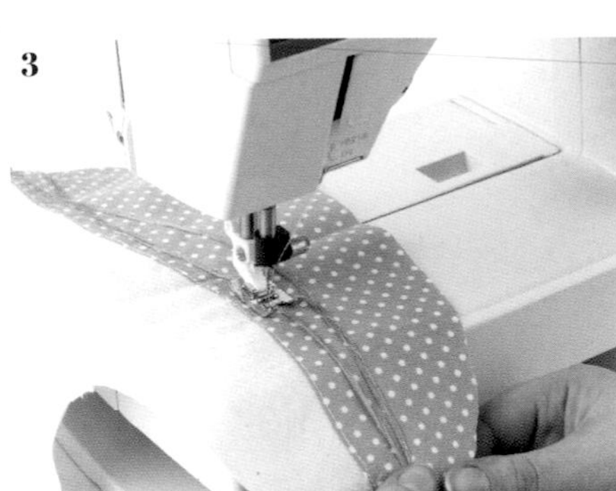

4

SIZE: 40CM (15¾IN) SQUARE, NOT INCLUDING FRILL

LEVEL OF DIFFICULTY

YOU WILL NEED

FABRIC:

- red cotton with large roses:
  1 piece 22 x 22cm (8¾ x 8¾in) for the front;
  2 pieces 42 x 33cm (16½ x 13in) for the back;
  3 pieces 10 x 110cm (4 x 43¼in) cut on the bias for the frill
- red cotton with small roses:
  2 pieces 5.5 x 22cm (2¼ x 8¾in);
  2 pieces 5.5 x 30cm (2¼ x 11¾in)
- pink and white patterned cotton:
  2 pieces 23 x 23cm (9 x 9in)

ADDITIONAL ITEMS:

- red and white checked bias binding, 2.5m (2¾ yards)
- white lace trim, 1m (39½in)
- jar, approximately 8cm (3¼in) in diameter
- pillow pad, 40 x 40cm (16 x 16in)

Frilly Pillow

PILLOW

1 For the front, sew the strips of fabric patterned with small roses around the centre square (see below, left). Neaten all the seams with zigzag stitch.

2 Cut the two squares of the pink and white patterned fabric in half diagonally to make four triangles for the corners. First sew two triangles to two opposite sides (see below) and then the remaining two to the other sides. Stitch the white lace along the edges of the central square, making a mitre in the corners.

3 Round off the corners of the front of the cover using the jar as a template.

4 To make the envelope closure on the back of the pillow, fold over a double hem of 1cm (½in) along one long edge of each of the back pieces and topstitch. Place the two back pieces together, with the hemmed edges overlapping to make the back the same size as the front. Pin them together then round off the corners in the same way as before.

5 To make the narrow frills on the front of the pillow, iron the bias binding open and cut to a width of 1.5cm (¾in). Sew along the strip then pull the threads to gather (see page 27). Sew the narrow frills onto the seams between the triangles and the red border around the centre. At the end of the seam, cut off the strip close to the edge of the fabric.

6 For the broad frills around the edge of the pillow, take the three bias-cut strips and sew them together to make one long strip (see page 20). Cut the strip to a length of 3.2m (3½ yards) and sew the short ends together to form a 'tube': fold the strip in half, wrong sides together, and gather it along the open edges to fit the circumference of the pillow (see page 27).

7 Pin to the front of the pillow, right sides together. Sew close to the edge. Place the pillow back on top with the right sides together and the broad frills tucked safely inwards and out of the way, then sew all around the edge.

8 Neaten the edges with zigzag stitch. Turn through the pillow cover and iron. Stuff with a pillow pad.

SIZE: 130 x 100CM (51 x 39IN)

LEVEL OF DIFFICULTY

YOU WILL NEED

FABRIC:

- cream cotton to make 95 hexagons and 7 half-hexagons; 11 x 10cm (4¼ x 4in) per hexagon
- assorted coloured cotton to make 51 hexagons and 7 half-hexagons; 11 x 10cm (4¼ x 4in) per hexagon
- brown cotton to make 7 hexagons; 11 x 10cm (4¼ x 4in) per hexagon
- black cotton to make 2 half-hexagons and white cotton to make 2 half-hexagons; 11 x 6cm (4¼ x 2¼in) per half-hexagon
- terry towelling fabric for the backing, 130 x 100cm (51 x 39in)
- black felt scraps

WADDING/BATTING:

- lightweight, 130 x 100cm (51 x 39in)

ADDITIONAL ITEMS:

- 5.5m (6yd) of bias binding, 2.5cm (1in) wide
- cutting mat, rotary cutter and ruler
- templates, see page 203

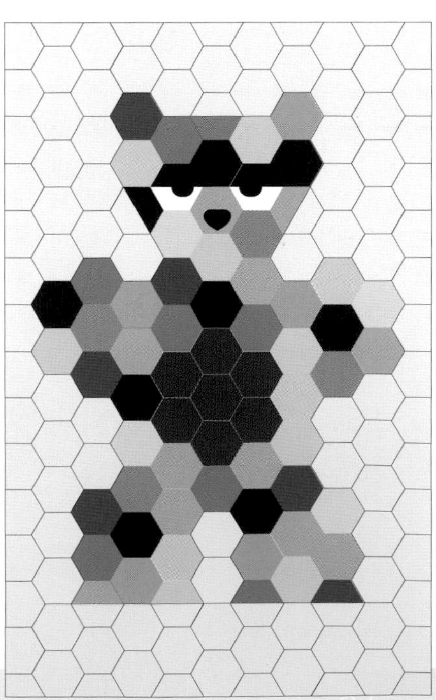

Baby Play Mat

1 Cut out and prepare the hexagons and half-hexagons in their corresponding fabrics and tack/baste them onto the paper templates (see pages 24–25).

2 Use whip stitch to join the pieces together, following the pattern in the diagram below left. I find it easiest to lay out the whole design and sew in small manageable sections, then stitch these together to assemble the finished design.

3 Remove all of the tacking/basting threads and release the papers from the back. Press the work flat using a steam iron and cloth to prevent any scorch marks. Trim the sides of the play mat to form a neat rectangle using a cutting mat and rotary cutter.

4 Lay out the towelling fabric and place the patchwork front on top. Pin the layers together to secure. Use the patchwork as a template and cut out the towelling. This will form the backing to the mat. Repeat this step to cut the same shape from wadding/batting. Sandwich the wadding/batting between the play mat top and backing, with the right sides of the front and back facing out. Pin the three layers together to secure.

5 Finish the play mat by trimming the edges with bias binding (see page 21). Machine stitch one side of the binding into position 1cm (½in) away from the raw edge. Follow the instructions on how to achieve perfect mitred corners. Fold over the remaining side of the bias tape and hand stitch this to the reverse of the play mat using matching thread. Use the sewn machine line as a guide.

6 Using the templates provided, carefully cut out the the teddy's nose and eyes using some scraps of black felt. Pin these into position.

7 Slip stitch the eyes and nose to the play mat and it's ready for baby to play on!

Geograph über dessen Moralität
uchung anstellen.«
her, der lügt, in den Geographie-
phen herbeiführen würde. Und auch
zuviel trinkt.«
gte der kleine Prinz.
fer doppelt sehen. Der Geograph würde
ge einzeichnen, wo nur ein einziger
Doch wenn die Moralität des For
man nachsehen?«
n. Das ist zu umständlich. Aber man verlangt vom
er, daß er Beweise liefert. Wenn es sich zum Bei
um die Entdeckung eines großen Berges h
ngt man, daß er große Steine mitbringt.«
lötzlich ereiferte sich der Geog
»Und du, du kommst vo
her! Du wirst mir de
Und der Geograph
spitzte seinen Bleis
Zuerst notiert
Bleistift. Um sie
bis der Forscher
»Nun?« fragt
»Warum das?
»Weil die Blu
»Was heißt
»sind die wertvollst
nie. Es ist

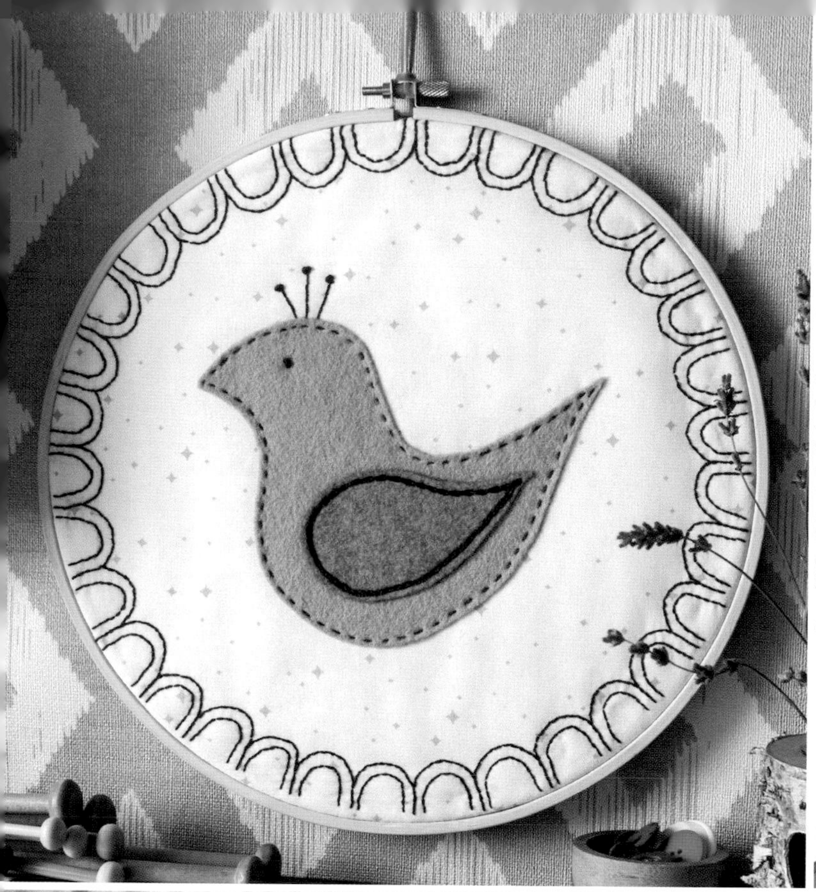

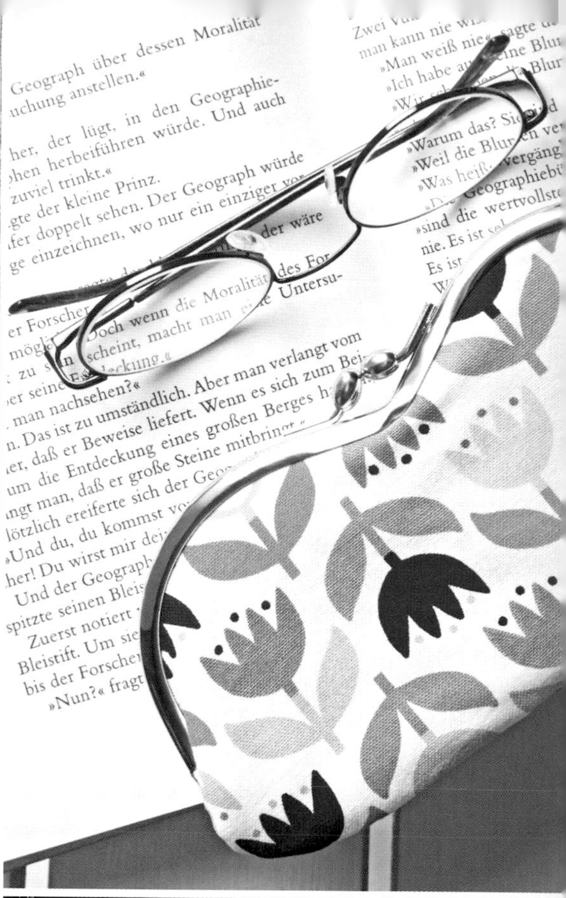

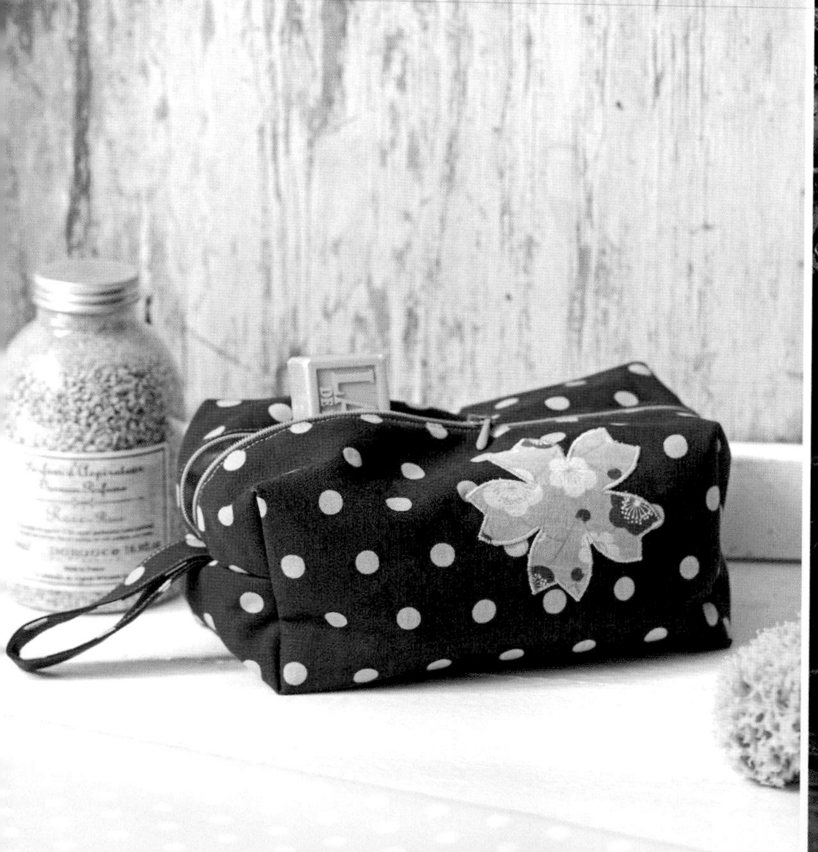

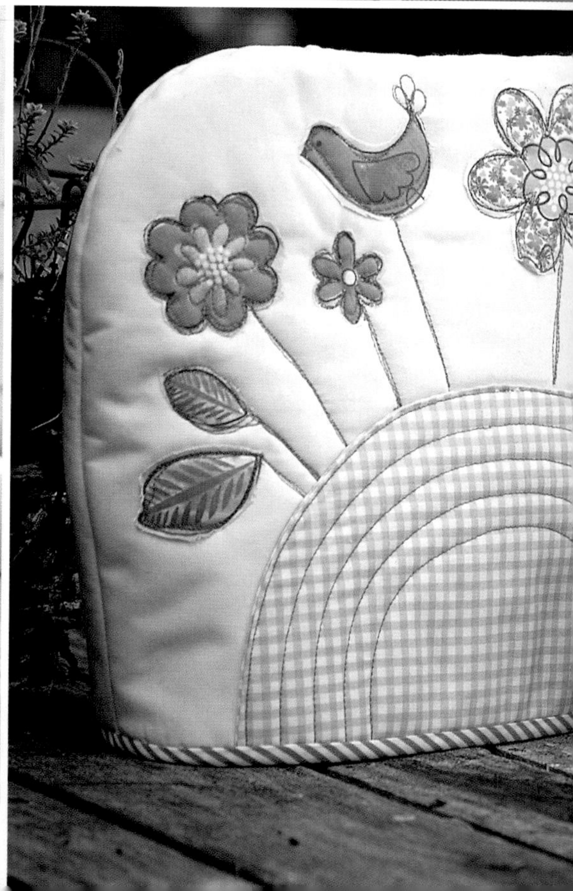

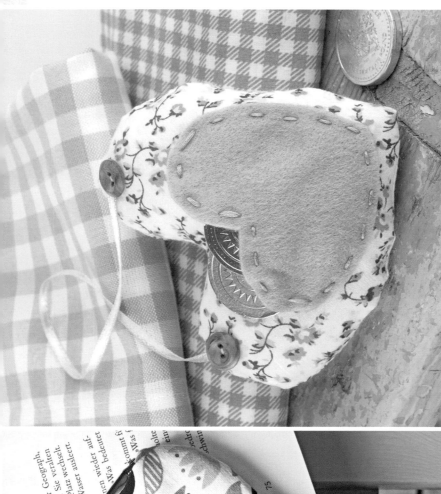

The templates

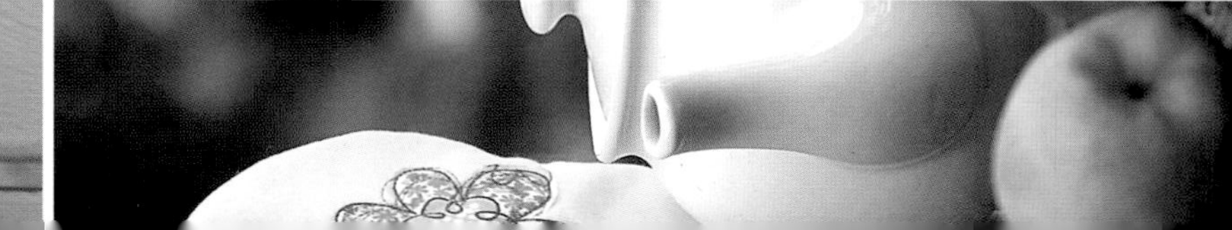

NOTE:

Most of the templates are shown at actual size; where this isn't possible, the percentage size shown is given so that you can enlarge the template.

Make-up Pouch

see pages 30–31;
shown at 50 per cent of actual size – print out at 200 per cent

Love Hearts Mug Hug

see pages 38–39

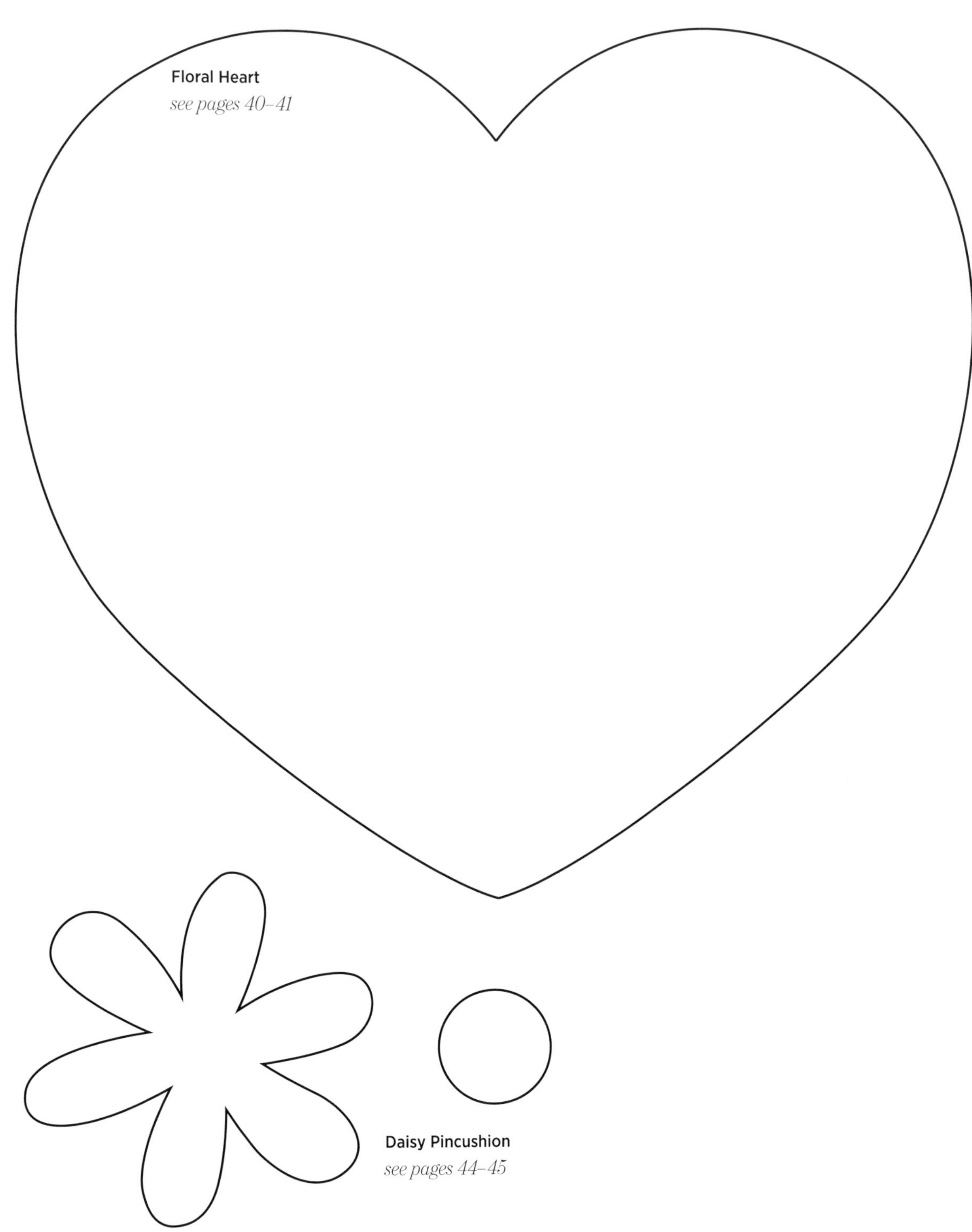
Floral Heart
see pages 40–41
Daisy Pincushion
see pages 44–45

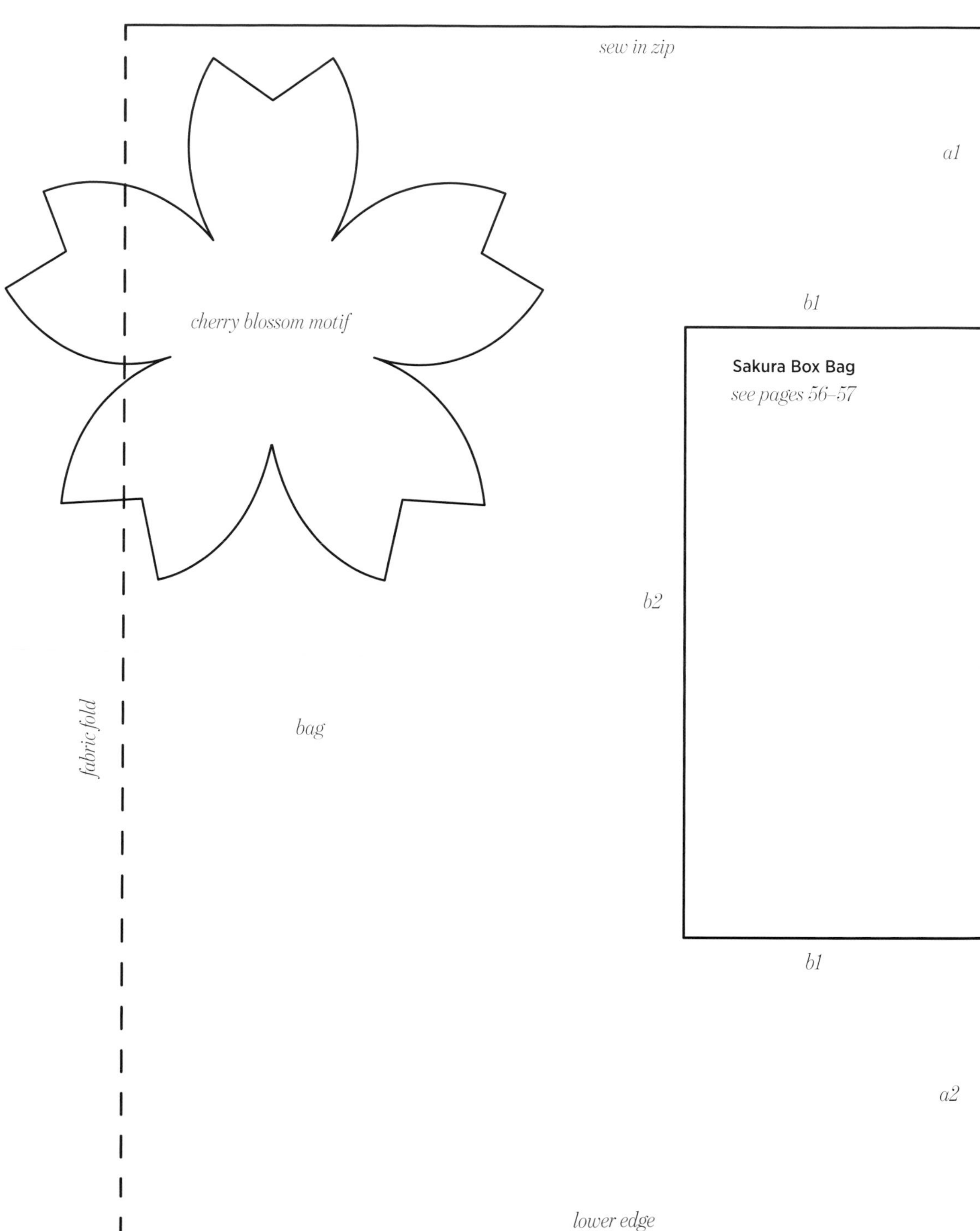
sew in zip
a1
cherry blossom motif
b1
Sakura Box Bag
see pages 56–57
b2
fabric fold
bag
b1
a2
lower edge

Pencil Case

see pages 42–43; shown at 50 per cent of actual size – print at 200 per cent

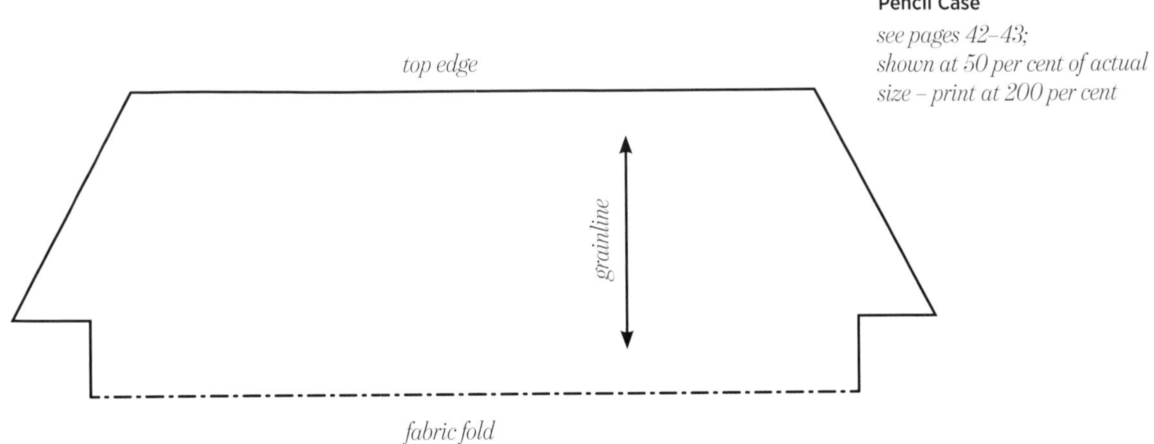

Hoop Art

see pages 58–59; shown at 50 per cent of actual size – print at 200 per cent

Allium Tea Cosy

see pages 66–67; shown at 50 per cent of actual size – print at 200 per cent

Summer Bag

see pages 72–73;
shown at 50 per cent of actual size – print at 200 per cent

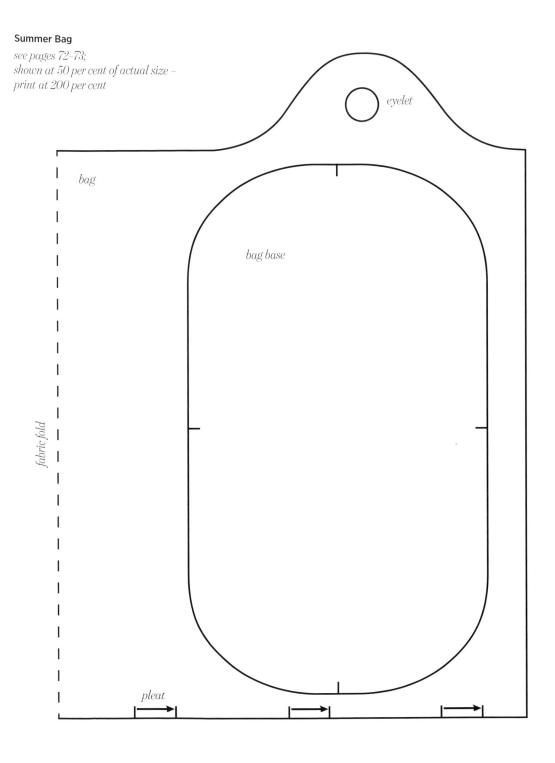

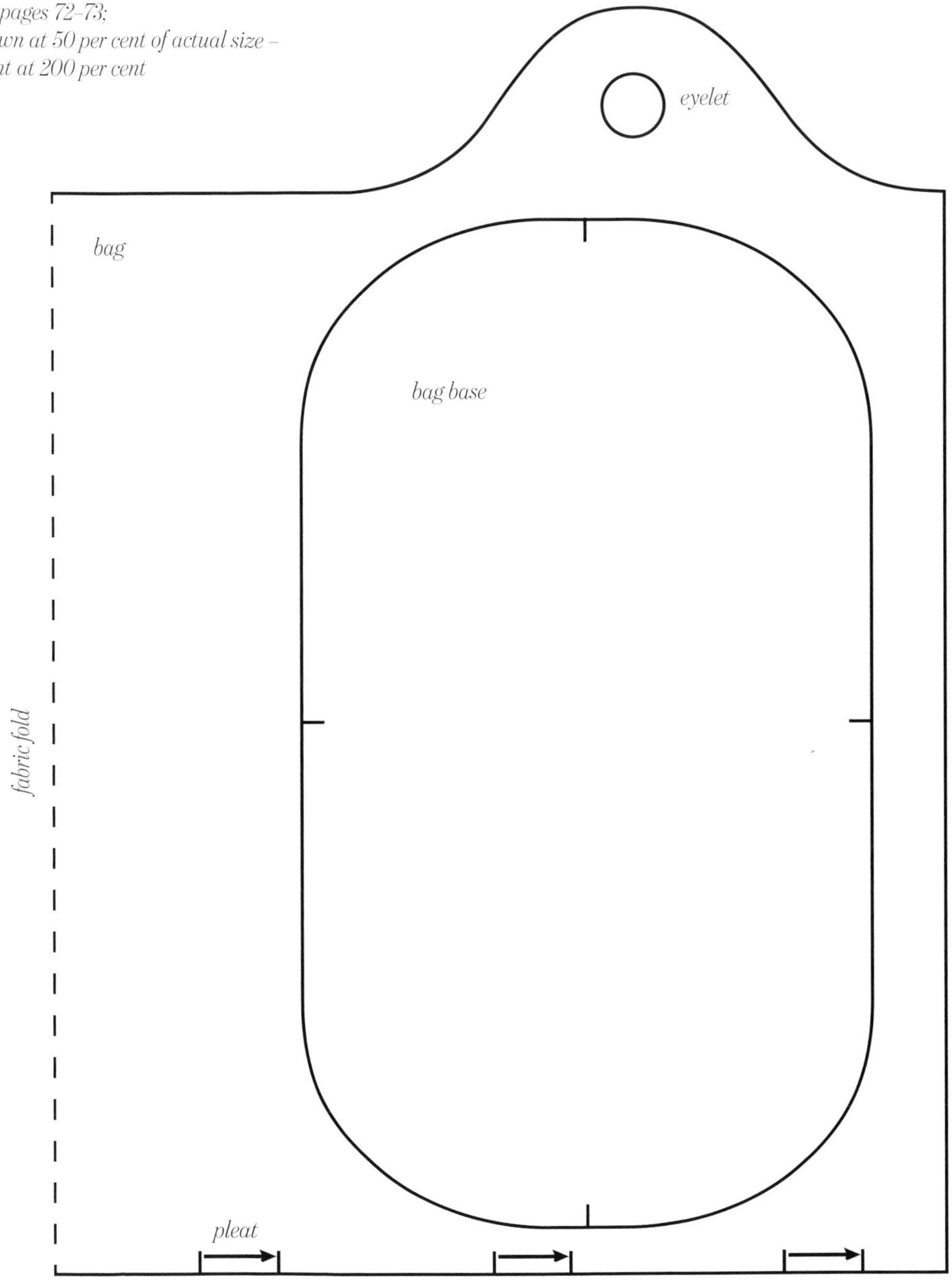

eyelet

bag

bag base

fabric fold

pleat

Apple Kitchen Set

see pages 86–89;
shown at 50 per cent of actual size – print at 200 per cent

Fun and Flirty Bag

see pages 90–91;
shown at 50 per cent of actual size –
print at 200 per cent

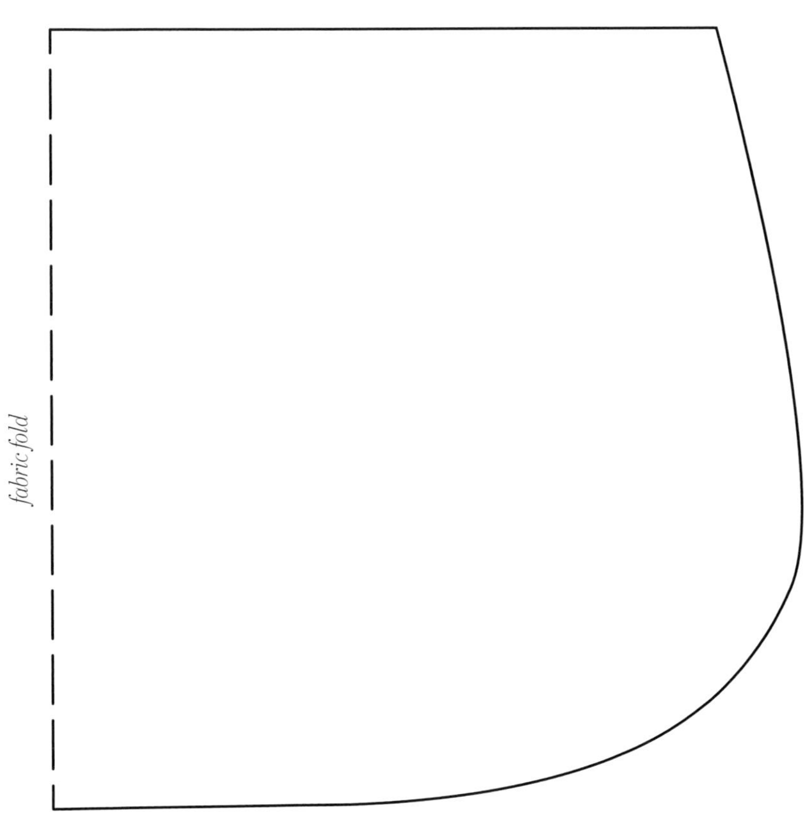

Nostalgic Charm Mug Rug

see pages 92–93

Flower Tea Cosy

see pages 94–95

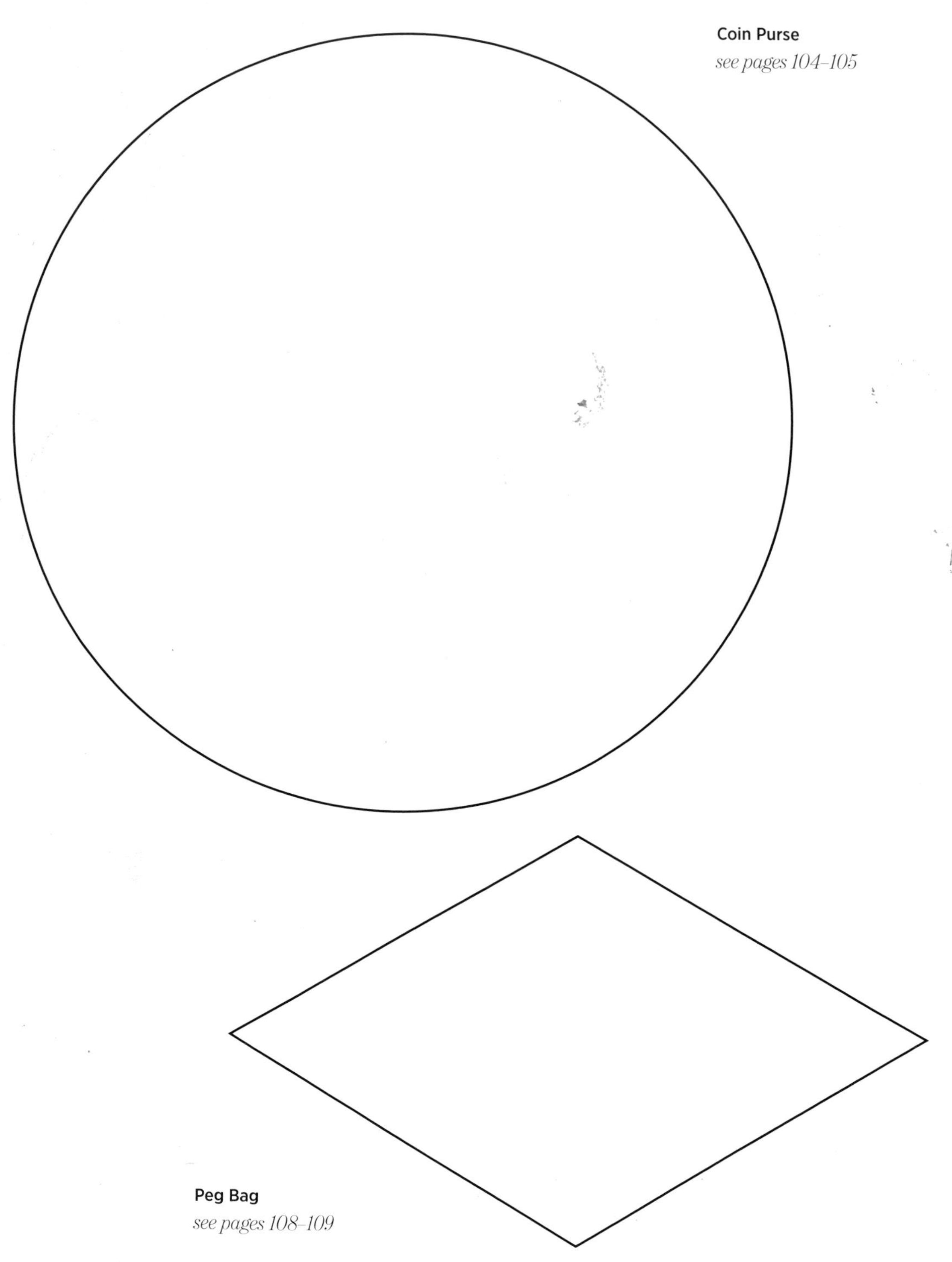
Coin Purse
see pages 104–105
Peg Bag
see pages 108–109

Button Heart

see pages 106–107

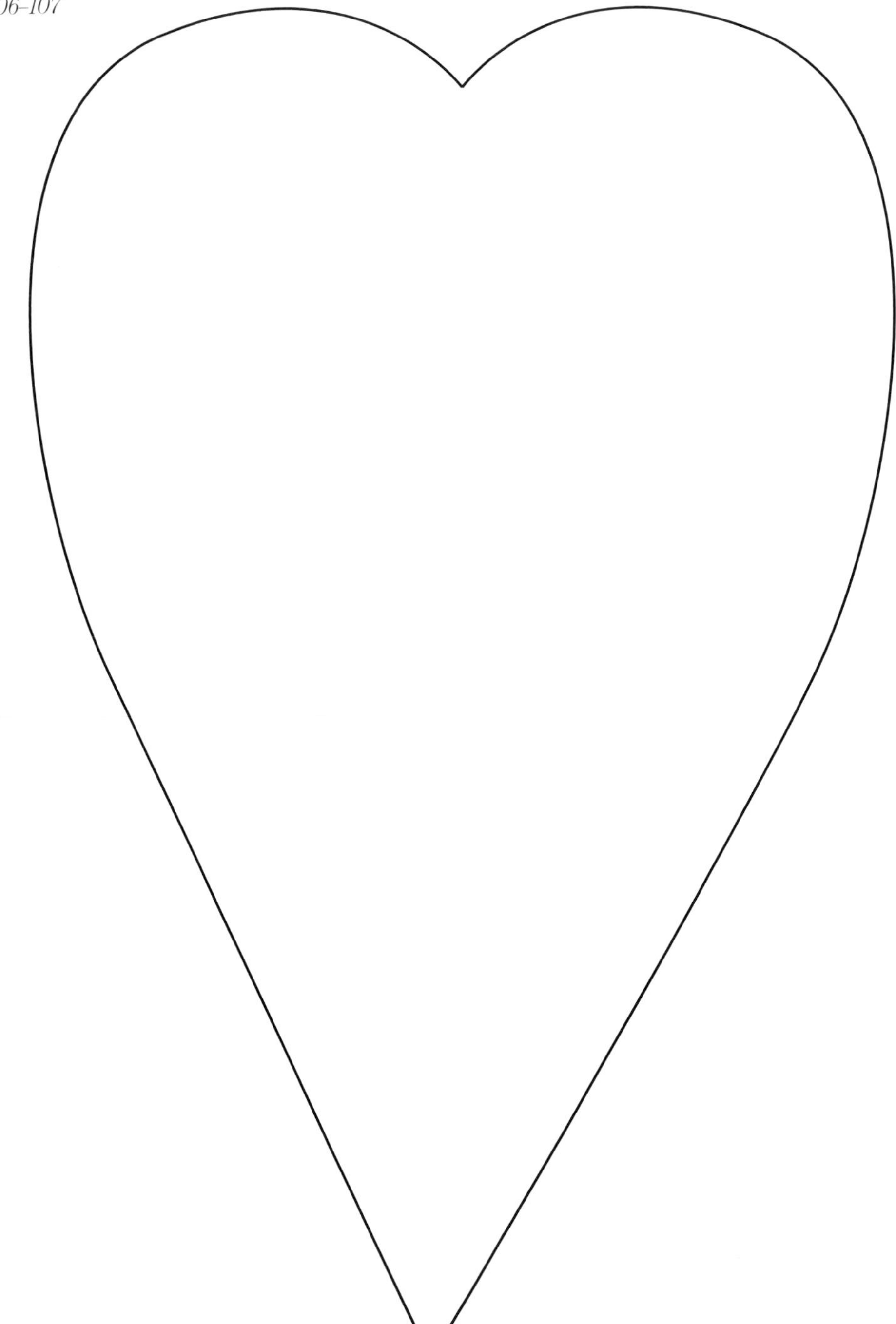

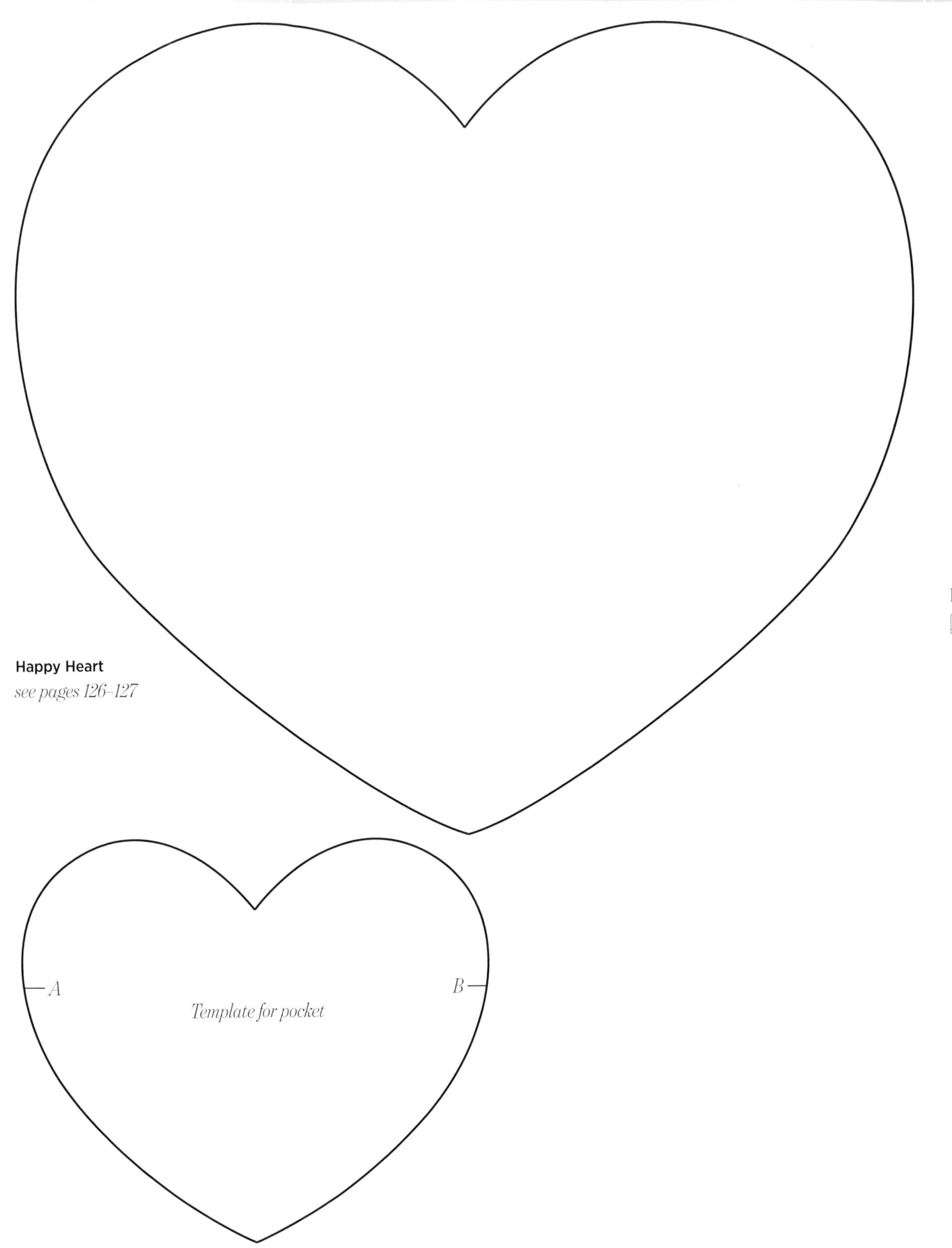

Happy Heart

see pages 126–127

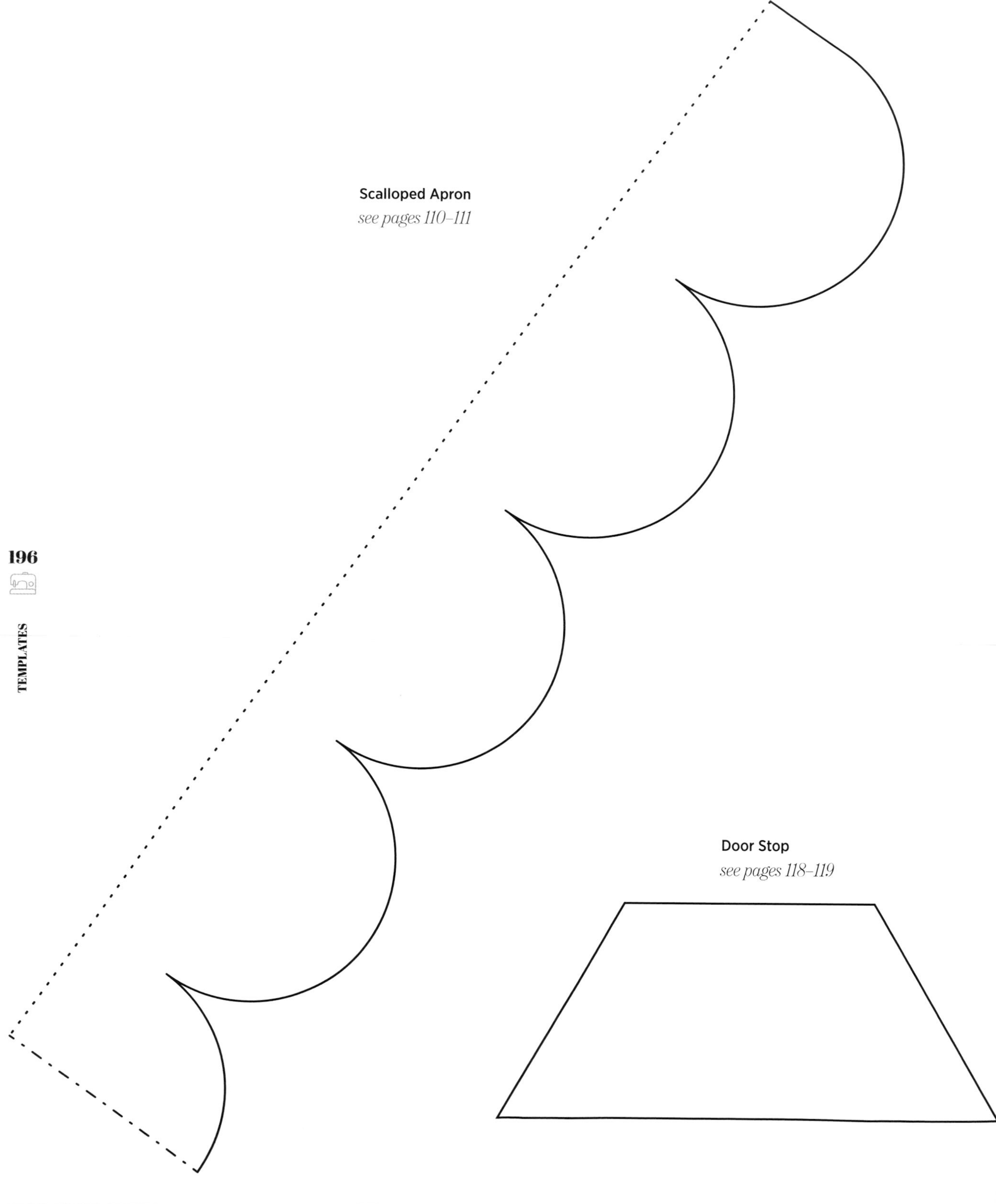
Scalloped Apron
see pages 110–111
Door Stop
see pages 118–119

Horse Hanger

see pages 128–129; both elements shown at 50 per cent of actual size – print at 200 per cent

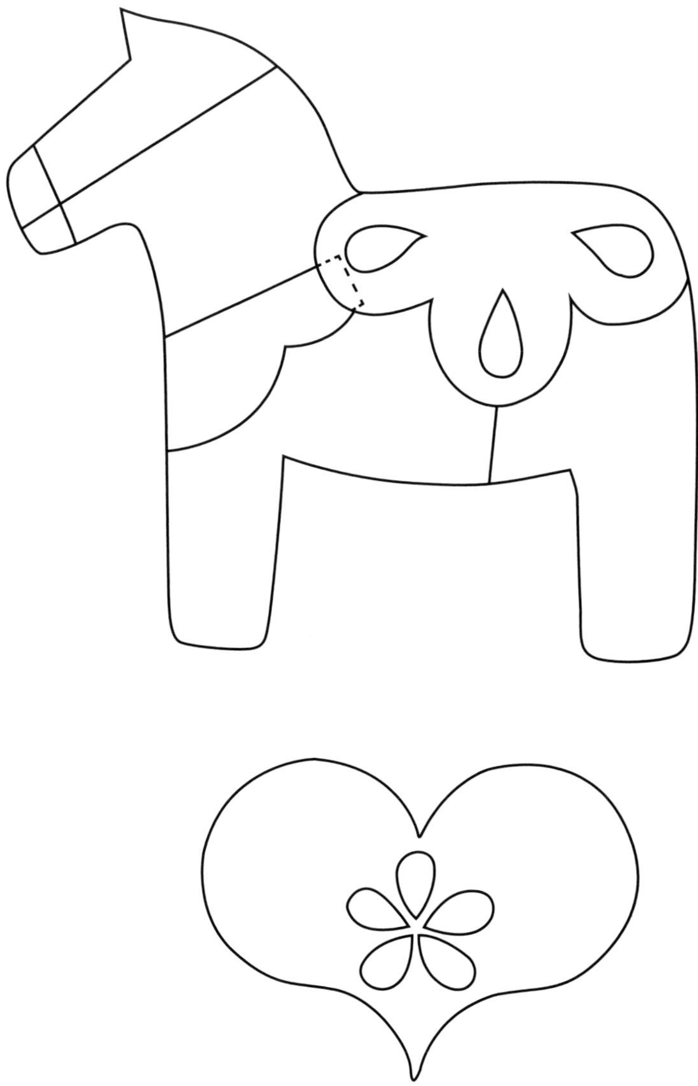

Strawberry Make-up Bag

see pages 134–135

flap

fabric fold and grainline

bottom edge – sew rickrack edging here

front/back

fabric fold and grainline

Tape Measure Cover

see pages 154–155

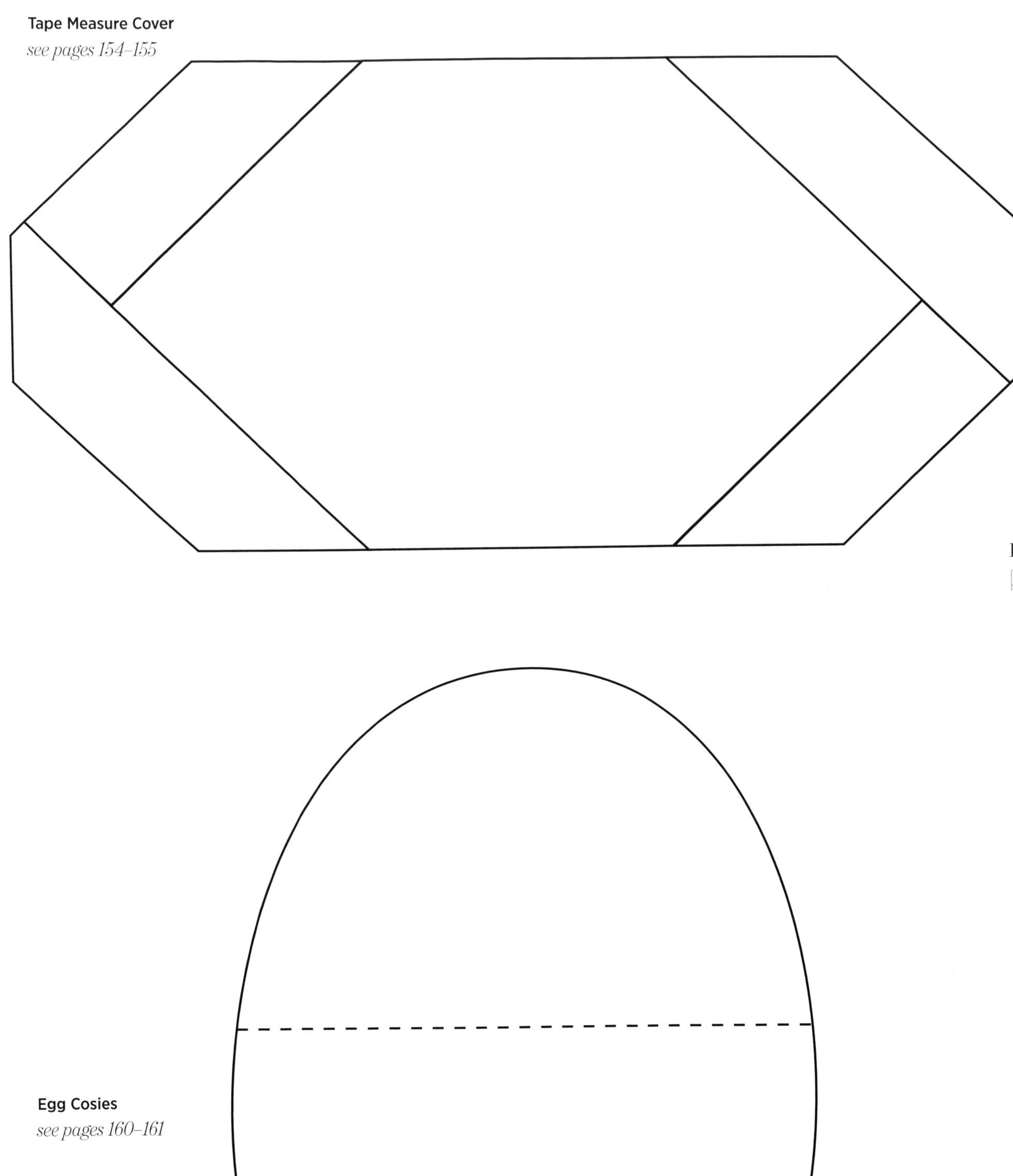

Egg Cosies

see pages 160–161

Diamond Make-up Bag

see pages 122–125

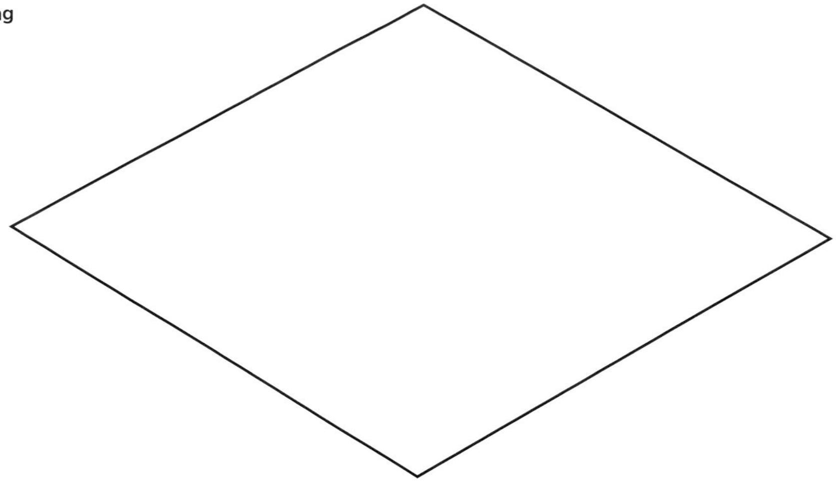

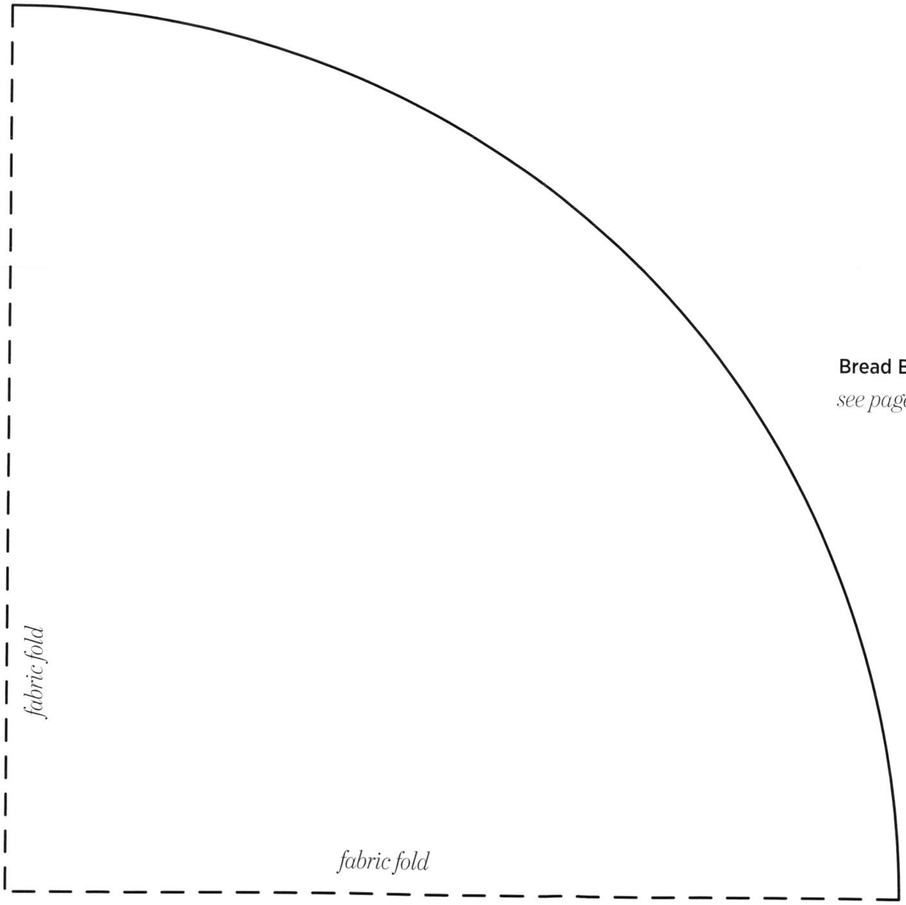

Bread Basket

see pages 138–139

fabric fold

fabric fold

Stockings Advent Calendar

see pages 168–169

Triple Layer Cake
see pages 162–163

*

fabric fold and grainline

Glasses Case
see pages 174–175

Baby Play Mat

see pages 180–181

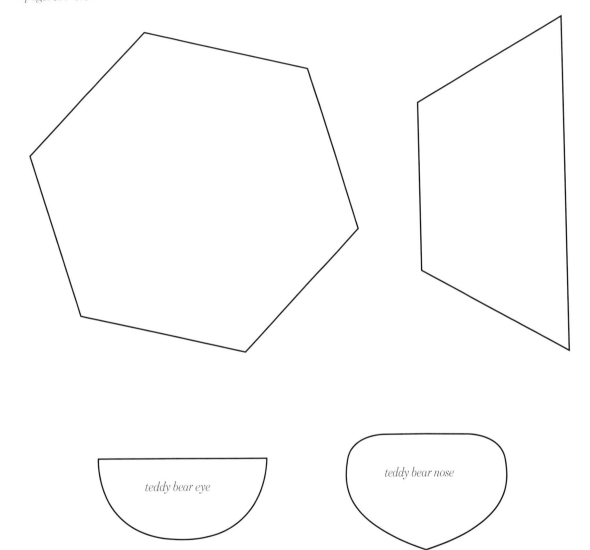

teddy bear eye

teddy bear nose

Appliqué Trees Stocking

see pages 176–177

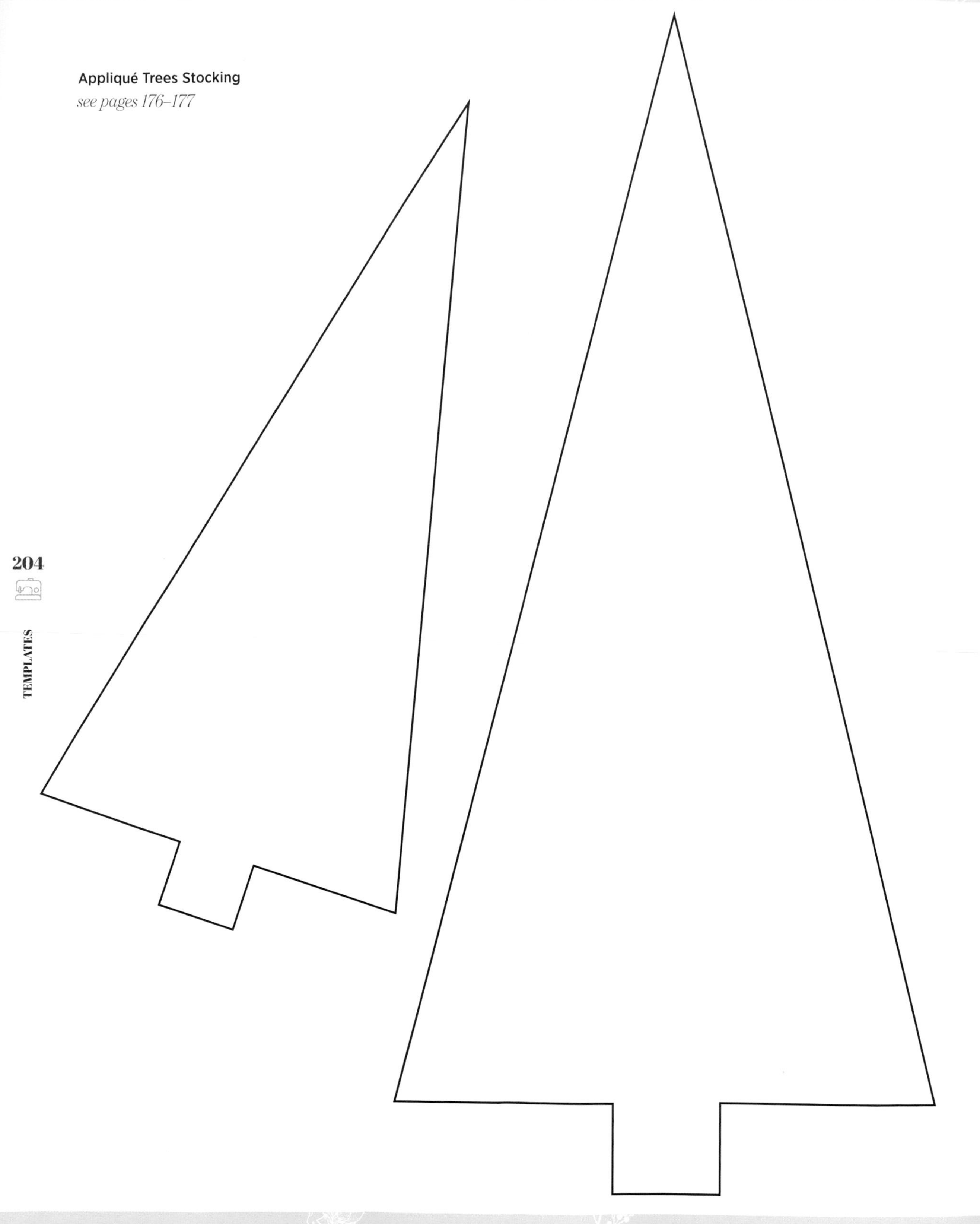

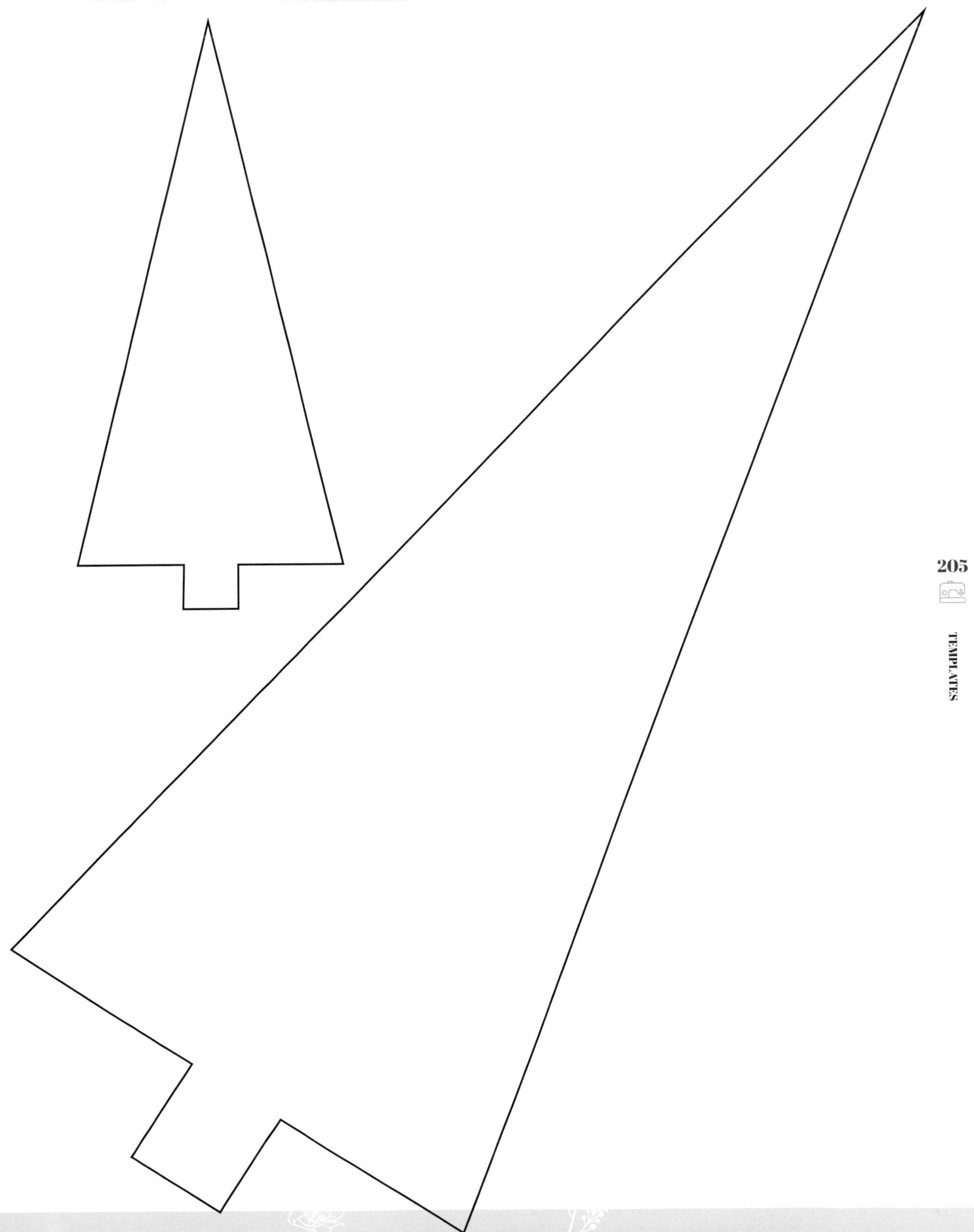

INDEX

Art. 300
1/2 Dtz.